Sex on Toast

T0160157

Tôpher Mills was born in Cardiff where he still lives. He left school at sixteen and went to work in a factory. Since then he has done many different jobs including; roadie, labourer, painter and decorator, market worker, plumber's mate, roofer, packer, shop assistant, designer, editor, publisher and journalist. He's traveled extensively around Europe and America and is an acclaimed writer/performer of his work.

A founder member of the Cabaret 246 group, he published ten issues of their magazine. He started the publishing company Red Sharks Press in 1983 and published 60 books of poetry and short stories. His writing has appeared in many magazines and anthologies and been performed in many venues and festivals both in the UK and abroad. He's also worked in radio, television and film and has written review columns for The Western Mail and New Welsh Review. His previous poetry books are, *The Bicycle is an Easy Pancake, Something's Awry, The Dancing Drayman* and *Swimming in the Living Room*. From 1997 to 2001 he was elected chairman of The Welsh Union Of Writers and in 2006 he won an Arts Council Of Wales Bursary Award.

Sex on Toast

Tôpher Mills

PARTHIAN

Parthian, Cardigan SA43 1ED www.parthianbooks.com
First published in 2021
© Tôpher Mills 2021
Editor: Jonathan Edwards
ISBN 978-1-912681-87-7
Cover image courtesy of William Dean Ford
Designed by Syncopated Pandemonium
Typeset by Elaine Sharples
Printed and bound by 4edge Limited, UK
Published with the financial support of the Welsh Books Council
British Library Cataloguing in Publication Data
A cataloguing record for this book is available from the British Library.

CONTENTS

ANGIN ABOWT

SOMETHING'S AWRY

BUILDING SISYPHUS BUILDINGS

TIDE MEMORY

WINTER CYCLING

INTRODUCTION

I never wanted to be a poet. I was quite happy to be a prose writer of the literary best-seller kind. However, having failed, at twenty, to get an agent, a book deal or the Nobel Prize, I got the idea that perhaps I was doing something wrong. In a booklet of extra-mural courses (night classes) I came across something called, 'Adventures in Creative Writing'. I hadn't even known such things existed. In my day there were no Creative Writing courses with degrees etc. Now they seem to be everywhere but then, even a creative writing extra-mural course was a rare thing. As I was unemployed I found I could get the course for half price so I signed up.

This was to be the act that most ruined my life and led me to become that hopeless thing called a 'poet'. I went along to the class with my short stories to find that just about everybody else there was a poet including and especially the tutor, Chris Torrance. Soon I was writing haiku and before long I was reading and writing poetry as if my life depended on it. To this day I do not fully understand what happened to me, just that I was hooked. I kept trying to resist until my poems started to get published and then a magazine called *Poetry Wales* actually paid me for a poem. All was lost.

I had known nothing about poetry except that I didn't like it. When I did learn about it I discovered that I not only liked it but was enthusiastic about it. I had been warned about getting too influenced by any one poet so I read as widely as possible. From Ted Hughes and John Tripp to Walt Whitman and William Carlos Williams among a host of others. I was, of course, influenced but usually only for a few poems before I moved on to the next poetic enthusiasm. Like most beginners I started out with free verse because it seemed easy. I soon discovered that writing good free verse was the hardest thing of all. Also I had trouble with traditional metrical verse as it seemed alien to me. The rhythms weren't Welsh or working-class and didn't come naturally to me. I found it strange that, for the most part, American free verse spoke more naturally to me

1

from the other side of the Atlantic than the Oxbridge poets from England. Many British poets had adopted the American idiom and applied it to British subject matter. This opened up poetry for writers like myself and enabled us to write whatever we wanted and gave us a valuable alternative to rhyming metre. I quite happily wrote and experimented with different forms as detailed in the section, 'Early Poems', which contains most of the early poems I wrote and published, but I was still searching for something. It struck me that the American idiom was American and I began to wonder if there was an English-language Welsh idiom.

One day I turned up to work as a roofer to find that the scaffolding, which should have been put up the day before, hadn't been put up. As we moped about wondering if we should just go home, the scaffolders arrived and said that it wouldn't take long to put up. So we went into the kitchen and had a cup of tea. As I sat there I listened to the scaffolders. They were from Ely, which probably explains why they were late, and they had broad, west Cardiff accents. At one point the comedian amongst them pretended to strike up a conversation with the Alsatian dog next door. When the dog barked he pretended to respond. It was very funny and we all laughed. It suddenly struck me that here was my idiom. Like William Carlos Williams writing in the idiom of Paterson, New York, I should write in the idiom of Grangetown, Cardiff.

During the next few years I listened to Cardiffians and tried to identify the traits of the Cardiff accent. As a Cardiffian, to talk Cardiff is easy but to write it down is much more difficult. I saw Tom Leonard, the Glaswegian dialect poet, reading his work and bought a book of his with a brilliant essay on dialect poetry that I learned a lot from and was greatly inspired by. The end product was the first Cardiff dialect poem ever written called, 'Nevuh Fuhget Yuh Kaairdiff'. Realising that very few people would understand a full-on Cardiff dialect poem I decided to evolve a poetry that used working-class Cardiff rhythms and speech patterns without having to write in dialect. I still wrote outside of that form occasionally, as certain poems demanded, but generally I became more and more at home with it. It was syllabic with a peculiar love of alliteration and a good deal of humour.

As someone who left school at sixteen, went to work in a factory and then did a number of manual jobs including a lot of roofing, I slowly became aware of how unusual I was in the world of poetry. Most poems about working-class life were written by middle-class poets who may have had a working-class upbringing but had very little experience of adult working-class life, work or sensibility. At best you would have a nice visual description of a building site or a dole queue usually written from a distance. You never got to feel what it was like to be that person either emotionally or physically. When I started writing about such things I realised I had very little poetical precedent and so I chose to write in a simple no nonsense style that wouldn't alienate me from my subject matter. I also chose to focus mainly on the kinetic and narrative elements of the poetry. These factors eventually merged happily with the Cardiff idiom to produce most of the poetry in this book.

A month after my first major collection came out, desperate for some sort of response, I pestered Peter Finch, the manager of Oriel bookshop and all-knowing in these areas, about what, if anything, people thought of it? He reluctantly let on that there was a suggestion that I had been 'aping Welsh-language poetry'. Knowing nothing about Welsh-language poetry I asked what he meant? He pointed me to the introduction by Anthony Conran in *The Penguin Book of Welsh Verse*. I was amazed to find that these Welsh-language poets wrote syllabically and rhymed along the line alliteratively. Not only had they ripped me off but they had the cheek to have done so over a thousand years before I was born! I soon realized the obvious, that even Cardiff, in its working-class areas (because they weren't educated to speak 'properly'), still retained some of its Welsh language speech patterns. That in spite of that awful period between 1914 and 1964 when, in a mere 50 years, Welsh speakers declined by 40% and the Welsh language suffered a kind of linguicide, traces of it would be left behind even in Cardiff. Like a glacier moving back across the landscape, leaving its mark in valleys and ridges so that, though it is no longer there, its effect is undeniable. This kindled an interest in Welsh-language poetry and then Welsh history that has greatly strengthened my own Welshness.

From the beginning I was encouraged to perform my work. The idea that language is a thing of sound and closer to music than to writing seemed only too apparent. Having started out as a writer of text, the secondary medium of language, I found this difficult at first. Most poetry came to me from books and, being shy, getting up in front of an audience was extremely nerve-racking. Being in a group of poets/writers performing their work greatly helped me. Being one of many meant that if I didn't go down well then the whole night wasn't ruined. Just having to do a few minutes also helped take the pressure off. The best thing about being in a group was seeing the varied ways other, better readers handled an audience. I learned a great deal from my fellow performers and overcame my shyness to the point where I started to actually enjoy reading my poetry and stories in public. I also started publishing small magazines and pamphlets. I didn't just want to be a performance poet, I wanted my poetry to work on the page as well, even though these two areas of poetry pulled in opposite directions. Part of the challenge was to make them work in both areas though I'm aware that I often veered one way or the other. It is a challenge I am still working on.

The poems in this selection are chosen from forty years of work. They are roughly in chronological order of writing, and I mean very roughly. The first section, Early Life, has new and old poems in it, but all about childhood. The second section, Early Work, has the earliest poems I wrote with one or two exceptions that ended up in the next few sections. In other words I have tried to put together a collection that flows and gives some idea of how my poetry has developed so far and, though my path does occasionally seem haphazard to say the least, I see this as a blessing not a curse.

The entertainer Ken Dodd once asked me, very seriously, 'What is Poetry?' The best answer I have been able to come up with, and this is just my definition, is that poetry is the sound and meaning of language combined in such a way as to transcend both.

Tôpher Mills

EARLY LIFE

APRON

My mother had a string of men
who phoned her days and evenings.
They'd ask briefly after my father, Ken,
who was never in, and then
they'd want to know what she was cooking.
She'd tell them in great detail, explaining
the recipes, why the ingredients,
what they did, how to concoct them.
She could whip up, ad hoc, in fun,
something on the spot, her instincts
for the delicious absolute, unwavering.
A platinum blonde of the kitchen,
she'd tell them what it looked like,
how it tasted, the texture, what it went with,
and these men, whose wives could barely open
packet mash, hung on every word, lingering
ears sweat-sealed to the receiver, salivating.

NOT WAVING BUT CAPSIZING

My father's head is bobbing expertly,
held several feet above sea level
by the oversized tartan life-jacket.
His arms flounder and splash ineffectively
because of an over abundance of buoyancy.

Too young to realize the danger,
we stand on shore in short trousers and leaky daps,
giggling as the wind ruffles our cropped hair.

Careening on the keel his feet dance
a jig of desperation as his hands jerk,
trying to jolt upright the unsinkable dinghy.
Like a magic trick its mast rises
in a shower of wind-ripped spray
and he half jumps, half falls in
with an incredibly deft awkwardness.

He sits up flabbergasted, then sees us,
leaping up and down the slipway, cheering.
He smiles, as if he'd never had a moment's doubt
and, while waving back at us, while bailing out,
the boat tacks and the boom swings about.
My father's head is bobbing with the impact.

A CHILD'S CHRISTMAS IN CARDIFF

    I WANTS A BMX BIKE!
    I WANTS A BMX BIKE!
    I WANTS A BMX BIKE!

aan iss krissmuss morning
aan gess wot?

    I GORRA BMX BIKE!
    I GORRA REEL BMX BIKE!
    I GORRA BMX BIKE!

aan duh furst fing I dus on it
is I tayuks ir owt duh layun
aan I doos dis faaantaaastik weeelie
aan I forls orf
aan I lans on mi bum
aan I urts myself
aan I kries
WAAAAAAAAAAAAAAAAAAAAAAAAAAAAA!
aan mummi kums aan gets mee
WAAAAAAAAAAAAAAAAAAAAAAAAAAAAA!
aan kaarrees mee baak in dee ows
WAAAAAAAAAAAAAAAAAAAAAAAAAAAAA!
aan kudduls mee
WAAAAAAAAAAAAAAAAAAAAAAAAAAAAA!
aan kissus mee bettur
                    YEEUURK!

Aaan now
I gorra BMX bike
                    fuh sayul!

ST. STANLEY OF THE LIGHTS

He was a nutcase we all knew.
If he saw you without
he would stop you and provide.

There would be no arguing
he could be very stern
and we were only children.

He was fast, within minutes
our way was lit front and back
safely fixed and no excuse.

There were some who conned him
got more light than they should
but that was rare because Stanley

remembered children's faces
had a knack for winkling lies
from the straight look of truth.

Some riderless bicycle chained up
without lights would be with them
after his green van had passed.

I laughed at his stupid waste
though I was only too willing
to get what he had to give.

When my dad heard this
he clipped me and told me
not to cheek my elders.

Then he told of Stanley
before we were born
a son killed by a lorry.

No lights on his bike
driver hadn't seen him
Stanley never the same since.

All Grangetown knew of him
though he is long gone now
and his devotion discontinued.

How many lives did he save
desperately haunted by the one
lost and left forever in darkness?

CHILD AT SKER POINT

Swimming out
to where the surfers sit
astride the large-beaked
bobbing surfboards
waiting for the perfect
one in every seventh wave.
I envied them.

When I'm old enough
dad has promised
a board and wetsuit
to ride the roller coaster
hump-backed sea.

Now I just swim confidently
long strokes slicing and pulling
legs kick propelling, cutting
through the playful green
and foam-flecked element.

Up to my chest
a kid splashing fun
jumping the high rollers
diving into them
feeling them slap me
as I surge through.

Caught unaware
the big wave surprises me
undertowed off balance
it hurls me under
tumbles me chaotically.

Panicked, fighting
arms and legs swirling
grabbing at white water
unable to right myself
mouth full of liquid fear.

Gripped powerfully
immense wave mass swept me
twenty yards of choking
towards blistered rocks.
Then it releases me.

Sputtering, disorientated
coughing water, gasping air
staggering, controlling panic
I stride drunkenly to slump
in damp, shell-wracked sand.

Wheezing, gulping, I sit up.
Far out surfers rise and dip
on the carousing ocean
which has tossed my confidence
aside with such awesome ease.

Raw throat tasting salt
squinting at the enormous
undulating and shimmering
I nervously comprehend
the scale of its challenge.

PETROL

Vomit streaking the car's white panels
nausea like damp metal, chewed wood
every turning is stomach churning
petrol fuming my senses, lost.

The back seat in the middle
furthest away from the big car's window
I learned about travel sickness the hard way
my father's rage hurling it into bends.

Continuously drizzle-ridden day-trips
to aerodromes, boat shows and shooting fairs.
The shotgun's jerk, the water's swell
or the Red Arrows lunging blast.

A squinting small boy, hair skew-whiff
atop a gleaming fighter plane
glare in the camera lens
hand over the eyes, a salute.

At best it was windswept beaches
hide and seek in castles or fruit picking
blackberrying with bows and arrows
filling up with strawberries to spew.

Three brothers, legs sticking to car leather
scrumped apples, laughter, tricking bitterness
rolling around our kicking feet
hurling them out the speeding windows

at the unsuspecting pedestrians
giggling at the delicious thwack.
"I'll bloody do you lot in a minute!"
Lost parents rowing, dad revving.

DIEPPE

Leaky tented
damp sleeping bags
here for a week of foreign rain.
Playing at soccer
with scouts from Croydon
we all yell and shout
punting the ball, the horde charge
everyone of us know-alls.

Holding onto door handle
feet evenly placed
on plateaued footprints
of white china, no lavatory
just strain and aim into
one small hole in the floor.
Wipe and step out quickly
as the flush metamorphoses
toilet to swimming pool.

Pillboxes
cliffs pockmarked by war
wind and pebbles camouflaged
the colour of concrete
the lumpy sea the same
weather as bad as Wales
sat in the Norman cold
awaiting anything
even bombers.

UNDER CLIFTON SUSPENSION BRIDGE

My Uncle Bill was the only man ever to fly
a Spitfire under Clifton Suspension Bridge.
Strictly against the rules of course
but in the midst of World War II
he was merely given a stern 'ticking off'
after freely admitting he'd done it
simply because he'd always wanted to!

Think of this one mad act. Stand on the riverbank
as if you were a small boy in the nineteen forties.
All your dreams caught by that icon, a Spitfire;
curving, wings arced as if in slow motion,
able to pick out the gun holes, the insignia
and the pilot's smiling wave as sensually aloft
the plane swoops around the Avon gorge
and under a bridge with people at its railings.
Cheering, yes they are cheering, who wouldn't?
Just imagine being there for that moment
a rapture so intense it is indelible.
That stillness of the river and in the distance
the faint hum of a disappearing vision.

REACH

1.

Freestyle they swim
we breaststrokers watch.
Close to the water's level
their overarms like gull's wings
bent for the downward flap.
The slap of feet somersault turning
and they head back to us.
Too quickly they finish.
Nervous we approach the blocks.

2.

A final goggle adjustment
red and blue lanes undulating
converging at the deep end.
I bend, fingers below toes
look down and listen.
"ON YOUR MARKS!"
At the pistol's shot
my body explodes
the best take-off ever
torpedo under the surface
one stroke, arms first then legs
up, breathe and reach
pull back
reach
every stroke
reach
forget speed
the one who reaches furthest
wins.
We all reach
stretch ourselves across the pool.
I know I have it.

I woke that morning knowing
just one of those days.
Catch the bank on full reach
and turn
breathe in mouth
out nose.
I'm on my own, out in front
I sense it like the taste of chlorine.
Everything slows
I cease to race
my strokes glide
I reach endlessly
foam gurgles beneath me
red and white sliding past
my heart booming
surrounding everything
REACH
BREATHE OUT
PULL BACK
BREATHE IN
REACH
BREATHE OUT
PULL BACK
BREATH IN
REACH

3.

I am not there
as my body
surges to touch tiling
a too vivid film
water curling smoke
floating
floating
floating

BROGUES, CIRCA 1971

Standing in Cardiff central bus station
feet splayed in new black brogues
a few sizes too big for me to grow into
taken as new to the cobblers and re-soled
till they are as stiff and clumsy as clogs.

Wind abusing bright red ears, wheezing
through the concrete shelter's smashed glass
water dripping steadily from the broken light
I stand on the edge of dismal puddles
waiting without hope for fun or trouble.

Mates joking about the huge size of my feet
I mooch off to the station shop for pear drops.
Plodding back I see my bus pulling away.
Leaping the small concrete wall I race
knowing from experience I'll catch it.

Jolting duffel bag's cord cutting shoulder
thumping brogues clack clopping on tarmac
kids jeering laughter, shouts out bus windows
long-legged feet slapping me along at full tilt
among several other latecomers racing me.

Almost the last of them I gain the necessity
of a hand on the cold chrome handrail the
one big jump to the platform all I need but
as I take it, Ross Linguard leaps in sideways
knocking me, jarring my foot which slips.

My hand jams between rail and bus doorway
wrist caught, my feet fumble, fail to keep up.
Flailing chaotically, I tumble, twisting hand
terror explodes adrenalin and I tense up
bodily yanked as muscles reel me in.

Spun right around and dragged backwards
behind the speeding bus, I'm amazed to find
the shiny solid black brogues are skidding
sliding over the road beneath them and me
performing like a perverse version of skis.

Contorting myself around to face frontwards
knees bent, absorbing the juddering strain
I desperately swing up onto the platform
free my wrist from the bus rail's grip
and let my dash-dazed soul catch up.

Seated upstairs the sweat of fear pours out
like the condensation dribbling the windows.
New leather soles are scored and worn down
by the friction of my life sustained at speed
of failing and yet still getting away with it.

FACE DOWN

Panic connects without language
it sweeps the beach and people run
mothers call children out of the water.
An old man no-one can understand
is shouting hoarsely at the sea's edge;
their Spanish, my English and his pointing.
A man is bobbing fifty yards away
face down. I enter the water.
My mother urges me not to go
sharks are mentioned but, face down
he hasn't breathed or tried to.
At fourteen I've already been told
I could swim the channel.
I strike out, no-one else enters
I'm alone, face down, my strokes
arc above the waves.

Before I reach him he sinks.
I dive and, like sea mammals
my heart slows the deeper I go
conserving oxygen, face down
blue-black, murky-cold depth.
Something glitters and I grab it
my lungs tightening, mind blacking out
I pull him to the surface and gasp.
Hand under his chin I swim
a few come to meet me now
success can make people brave.

On the beach I go through the motions
clearing the throat, pumping the chest
and, strangest of all, the kiss of life.
Those cold lips, icy, breathless.
Nothing works, nothing moves
except the glitter of his watch.

Later I'm told he was Russian
that he'd had a heart attack
(there was no water in his lungs).
He was old, sunburnt, his body well fed
un-Russian somehow, even his watch
was expensively flat, slim and waterproof.
But those lips, puckered marble
I can feel them now, always
my first taste of death
cold as the Steppes in winter.

THE LAST DAY AT SCHOOL

It was a hot, languid, July day when we threw Paul Hicks' satchel in the building site cement mixer. It was so heavy when pulled out we had to drag it back to the playground where we left it oozing cold, grey lava.

All afternoon Hicks searched through cupboards and cloakrooms as we giggled and glanced out the window at the small mound rapidly drying in the mid-day sun.

With the rest of the day full of nothing to do the girls decided to have a snogging contest. We boys would have to snog them and they'd rate our capabilities accordingly. We boys had no say in this for if we didn't snog we would instantly be deemed as virgins. To us this was both a delight and a torment. To snog all the girls was great but to risk being rated as a crap snogger was a form of torture the girls seemed to get more pleasure out of than the actual snogging.

The girls then spent a lot of time (if only to prolong our agony) working out what was good and what was bad. It was alarming to us that they had far more ideas about what constituted a bad than a good snog. We boys never questioned for a moment where exactly their expertise came from, they were girls, they just knew.

This was proved when they announced to us that getting a stiffy while snogging them would definitely be a bad thing. How the heck were we boys, at sixteen, supposed to snog all the girls in class and not get a stiffy? In fact we all knew we'd probably have stiffies that lasted for days after snogging that lot.

When the snogging eventually started the adjudication system was rigorous enough but things soon got out of hand and by the end of the last lesson it was obvious that the rating system was no longer applicable.

When the last bell went the girls skipped out gleefully laughing and joking about us boys with our strange walks all trying to cover embarrassing protuberances with our satchels. All that is except for Paul Hicks, who had at long last discovered his satchel and was now trying to chip it free with a stolen toffee hammer.

NEVUH FUHGET YUH KAAIRDIFF

Fraank Fanaarkaapaanz on duh mitch
inis bestest daps
onis faastest underaang bogey
like uh propuh *Beano* comic

Mad Motters donkeyin
raaysin froo Grange-end gaardns
korzin uh wopin grate malaarkee
dodgin duh dideekoys

scraamblin kross duh daafs
kraakin jelly froo duh tyewlips
an nuh Paarkeez frowin uh woblee
totuley owta duh winda like

"BLUDY LIDUL DOWZOWS"
ee yelz all jottld up to is nodjem
"YEWUL GET SUM GROLUP YEW ERVA
PAARKS YUR AARS ROWUND YUR AGEN"

Motter mite be beejobuld
buh Fanaakaapaan ees norra dill
iss is dreem wen ee growz up
tuh bee obuldeeoy tuh duh kween

aan duh Paarkeez aad uh maajorum
is germojumz gon all maankee
"Faaraawaakin boluhwoks" ee baars
"iyum orf down duh skin ows"

aark aark duh laark
frum Kaairdiff aarms paark
iyull aav uh Klaaarksee pi
aan un aarf aan aarf uh Daark
aa aan
uh baanaanuh jaam saarnwidj

EARLY POEMS

THE FACTORY

1. THE TRAINEE

A trainee repairer under Ken (fag in mouth
thin, glasses, slicked-back hair RAF style)
dismantling lorry injectors
their holes cleaned, valves checked
then ground down or replaced.

Bolted onto the tester, oil is pumped.
If the pressure is right, if the valve works
you put a washer over the nozzle
bag it up and label it.

If it doesn't work, it's like any other job
you piss about until it goes right.
Finally you write it down in the book
so's when they come back
everyone knows who's to blame.

2. STANLEY

Stanley was a new boy's nightmare. Grey, permanently uncombed hair, chequered shirt, sleeves rolled up to the elbows, glasses askew; he could camp it up mercilessly. "OOO! I bet yours is huge! How about a feel then big boy?" Suspecting a joke but not quite sure, his effeminate act so well practised and played to the hilt. "Bet you're built like a stallion eh?" His mincing demolishing teenage sensibilities, backed me up against a wall. Everyone sniggering at my embarrassment as I tried to joke my way out of it, falsely falsettoing; "Help rape!" and then, "I'm being nobbled by a bum bandit!" To which Stanley's mouth dropped in mock shock. "OOO NOO! It's not your bum I want, it's your lovely big cock!" The rest of them doubled up at that, fell over themselves in hysterics and gave the game away. Luckily for me mid-morning break started then and the fun stopped because not even that was more important than tea.

Later I learned he was as over-the-top to everyone including the secretaries (to whom he'd make lewd suggestions and tell rude jokes) and was, of course, happily married. It was his appearance that did it, he was always being taken for something other than what he was. Once, while drinking after work in the Black Lion, he was asked to leave because, as they put it, "We don't want any gypsies in here."

3. OVERALLS

Slithering into overalls
feet first carefully
then re-arming ourselves
for work and whatnot.

Newly laundered
they feel good
stiff and material
a persuasion of protection.

At the week's end
the cloth is ragged
soaked with stains
it drapes all over.

First thing in winter
holding them up to the heater
arms and legs billowing
a second skin warmed.

In summer they're discarded
hardly used but laundered
for those that waist-tie sleeves
and the few worn no matter what.

Pockets and cuffs rip
buttons disappear completely
knees and elbows wear out quickest
crotches Yogi bear slowly.

We gad about in them
till the end of the week discards
these bulky uniforms of work
in a flattened corpseless pile.

4. SNOWJOB

Five minutes to eight and just on time. The wheels of my bike sliding on ice, having to put a foot down round corners, the pedals revolving too slowly because it's stuck in fourth gear. Upright, like I like it, sheepskin covered hands jerking the chopper handlebars steadily, my big ex G.P.O. Crombie coat that I swapped my brother my Parker for when I was in school (Jesus and I used to think school was boring), my bobble hat and well-wrapped scarf, with which I'm all done up like some big woolly ninja so why the hell are my ears still dropping off? I'm just taking it easy, going slowly, when this long load lorry turns left and I'm on the inside and trick wobbly over I fall and scramble and pull the bike clear as the lorry's back wheels mount the pavement to rev away leaving me sweating in the snow. Getting up furiously I see it stop down the road and start to pedal like buggery to catch. So rapt in annoyance and dreams of what I'll do to the driver as I pass along the lorry's length that only at the last second do I see the box van. The road isn't wide enough for me to squeeze through. As I brake, so does the van and we skid, my two wheels gliding awry till I hit it with a gentle thud that doesn't hurt. The foot-thick snow from its roof, however, avalanches over me and I become abominable. The lorry pulls away, its driver unaware and unconcerned. I reassure the van driver and recompose myself into a solitary cyclist who's now late for work. I turn my snow-capped bobble hat to the car behind me in which a family are hooting and wetting themselves. So another day begins.

5. BUFFING

The buffing machine cleans
the dirt, oil, rusted corrosion
of fuel injector metal to a shine.

Its wire brush discs send out sparks
fling bits to eyes, scuff fingers
leaving you raw and blinking.

Dig the nozzle deep into the pile
feel the jerk shuddering jolt up your arm
things are snatched, especially when small

spun away to leave knuckles hotly grazed
till all is dipped into the paraffin
to wash metal and cool hands.

6. MARTIN

Mad Martin 'farawackin bollawocks' Griffiths, always sniffing and joking around the secretaries, a boy with a cock for trouble and a nose to find it, warned me off the secretary with the great arse, "She's mine." I smiled being new and not knowing the score. Later we had a marathon joke-telling contest that went on all day, hurling them back and forth between us and as it went on the good jokes got bad, worse, diabolical; 'Jones the spy' 'Chewing a toffee' 'Everyone sings in Whales' and these the best of them. The other workers groaned louder with each joke. Neither of us won, it wasn't that sort of a contest, more like who could lose the worst!

7. DRILLING

I love to feel the drill bite
slowly rotating in the tri-handled levers
till coolant steams on hot metal
filings curl up, entwining.
Always that tension, concentration
to make sure the bit is on the mark
countersunk to stop the metal slide.

Once it smacked my hand, flung it away
the metal and drill bit hurtled across the floor.
When all was retrieved the drill was bent.
The others laughed at it, carbon steel bent!
I had achieved the impossible.
"Only you could have done that"
the boss moaned. It was almost a compliment.

8. SPANNER

Me and John are being told by the boss, "These are the ones, big order, all got to be done quick too." We look down at the ship's injectors, bloody huge things. "Where's the fork-lift truck then?" I ask and they both laugh.

So me and John wheel them on the widdy cart and then hump them, took both of us, although one of us could lift one if we really strained ourselves, buff them, dunk them in paraffin, clamp them in the vice and then jerk about on the big spanner's end trying to loosen the grime-ridden nozzles. Sweat running, cursing at awkward ones, the heat up in the hundreds, making it tell, I'm yanking the spanner with a pipe on it to extend the arm, get the most out of the leverage. I really wang it one and snap the spanner arm. "Who else but you?" John laughs, "Well you'll have to pay for it now," he kids me and it's my turn to laugh. A right herbert.

So me and the boss take the broken bits to the machine shop a few blocks down where a hunchback midget cuts a new one on a car-sized machine, coolant spraying around its hot edges. We wait as his skill finishes it in no time. Back at the rush job I'm just in time for tea. The lads take the piss out of me; "Here he is, Man of Steel." "Supertwat!" "Clark Kent's big sister." "The man who can bend his own erection." This latter is followed by a whoop from Stanley who slaps down a straight flush on the greasy table to a, "Jammy bastard!" "Oi!" shouts Stanley indignantly, "Less of the jammy."

Charlie the foreman bellows, "Come on you wankers." John quips, "Foreman! More like a bloody foreskin!" and we trudge back to the drudgery, the challenge that evolution has made for us. Me and John, over skilled and underpaid, pitting ourselves against lumps of inanimate metal.

PECKING ORDER

Silhouette horizon
one sun glip
peeking through
a crust of trees.

A yellow cloud
of roses
kites
tree strung.

Sparrow infantry
Bullfinch sergeants
figitly wait
respecting fear.

Young Blackbird
laser yellow beak
zapping
stale bread.

Cromwellian armour
polished gloss
gilt edged
smooth riveted
an officer.

WAAPN

"Waapn Mills?"

I often hear it
voiced at me
by a passing
vaguely familiar
Rastafari.

I usually fumble
my reply
    "Hello
    emm!
    Hi
    err!
    Waapn maan."

By my 'waapn maan'
the Rastafari
is aways away
down de street.

I always tink
I's mus lern
tuh bop bak
speedee liek
wid dee
"Waapn maan".

The hand is proffered
the plummy nasal voice
politely imparts
"Hello, how are you?"
"Waapn maan!"
sez I instant liek
an I giz im skin!

HOMAGE TO HENRY NORMAL

I remember when
I had love letters from the
Department of Social Security.
Assignations were made
for love I'd go anywhere
but fulfilment was elusive,
I started to suspect that what was wanted
wasn't me but my UB40.

Wary of being used
I turned up without it once
and was treated abysmally,
told repeatedly that I must
bring the beloved thing.
They were positively obsessive about it.

So I became reluctant, disenchanted,
hid my UB40 card and played hard to get.
I received letters wooing me back
promising big fat Giros
seductively suggesting the benefits.

Having a heart I relented
how could I resist
don't we all crumble in the face of it?
But I was haughtily informed
that it was too late, that I should
have made myself more available.

My Income Support was jilted.
All my pleas were rejected
and broken hearted, I'm dismal now.
I painfully learn how hard it really is
to love with insufficient means
in a cardboard box going soggy

with only half a bottle of Vimto
to console me as I tearfully read again
the Department of Social Security's
final Dear John.

THE DANCING DRAYMAN

It's raining and I'm blotto
dancing on wet aluminium
a drunken drayman
full of Christmas high jinks
on a lorry loaded with barrels.
In one complicated step
that would have made Astaire wince
I slip and, wind-milling, fall.
Sprawling in the road
brakes lock, tyres squeal
I get up laughing
you never hurt yourself
when drunk
only other people.

A SCHEME FOR LIFE

If you're available for work
you have to go on a scheme.
If you don't go on a scheme
you're not available for work
so you're not eligible for the dole.
The choices have been made for you
face up to the plastic window
life is doing what you don't want to.

So they stopped my dole
because I wouldn't do a scheme
I couldn't see the benefit of.
I wandered from office to office
being told to go nowhere
and going there to chew wallpaper
for three weeks until I gave in.

Bitterly I started in January
for the same money as the dole
I travelled 40 miles a day
there and back to Stormy Down, Pyle
which lived up to its name.

I was to make coffee tables
tools and wood provided.
Remembering the carpentry lessons
my father and my grandfather
the master shipwright had taught me
unaided I just went about it
enjoying the feel of the wood
proud of the finished product
but ashamed of the unpaid work.

On the bus we talked
some were serious about it

most were caught and angry
"How can we look for jobs
when we're stuck doing this all day?"
The inevitable drudgery of knowing
"And at the end of all this
when we go to sign on again
they'll want to know why
we haven't got a job after the scheme!"

We swap jokes, stories
and argue for something to do
rather than look out of the bus windows
at bleak landscapes of brown greyness
full of jobs being done, fleeting by.
Chivvying each other along
looking at page three as if…
There's talk of horses and bets
the possibilities and odds
as the pack is dealt on the back seat
but you can never win
not losing just isn't enough.

After eleven weeks of bloody coffee tables
any interest in carpentry has vanished.
The monotony of being ripped off
soon becomes an immovable splinter.
Hopes are confined to not too much
filling in forms and questionnaires
before some money comes
before they find another scheme
digging ditches in Cwmbran
filling in ditches in Cowbridge.

Face up to the plastic window
life is doing what you don't want to
and getting screwed for it.

PARK PLACE

Ramshackled in sunlight
the large faded house
stands out in the heat
prickles its neighbour's
tidy middle-class offices.

The door's an open invitation
we take for granted
it's our job
clean out, board up
make secure, and
unofficially of course
turf out the tramps.

One is rolled in an old carpet
asleep to our entry
the others having escaped
out the back quickly
without telling him.

Joe hits the floor with his shovel
"Cum on, lets be avin you."
The tramp burrows out
like a creature from the sea bed
                    a human crustacean.

"Oh dear
  sorry old man
  must have overslept
            eh what!"

The plummy nasal tone surprises us.
"I say, you chaps boarding up the place?"
Joe laughs
"Aye, you'll ave tuh find another kip."

The tramp scratches himself
plods towards the doorway.
"One is always having to find
a new residence in my game old boy."
We all laugh.

As we shovel
bottles, catalogues and excrement
into black plastic bags
we exchange jokes
and wonder why we
like servants
are cleaning up
        after him.

MARIE

She was seventeen and never knew
that I was only fifteen.

We'd meet in Alexandra Gardens
if it was raining in the museum
where we'd find a place to be alone
usually the mineral section.

It was a brief affair.
We never made love.
Just kisses, the arousal of close bodies
and the strain of nowhere to go.

We talked about death
my liking for Herman Hesse
her liking for Leonard Cohen
and the secrets of life
the usual teenage stuff.

She once said, very sternly
"I just want to help people."

Her parents, very strict Roman Catholic
rowed with her for not knowing
what to believe, for wanting
to get away.

As her bus pulled out for Llantrisant
she waved goodbye and blew
a kiss laughingly which was
unusual for such a serious girl.
I wondered what she was up to.

The gardens were empty without her
the mineral section just so much rubble
I wrote but she didn't reply.

For weeks I sat reading
watching the students sunning themselves
hoping she might turn up
and knowing she wouldn't.

***   ***   ***

'Stretching my legs' outside Trieste
the sea wind blowing salty dust
across the road rippled my shirt
cut into the perspiration on my back.
It was a last look at Italy
before crossing into Yugoslavia.

Opposite cliffs down to the sea
a high walled garden with open gates
and as I passed them she said, "Hello".

Despite my moustache and short hair
she'd recognised me but it took
a while before I knew.

We walked up the driveway
she refusing to let me help
push the man in his wheelchair.

Depositing him inside
she came back out with two 'Fantas'.

Drinking the sticky orange liquid
we talked of how she'd watched me
strolling downhill towards her
of seven and a half years past
when, after our last meeting
she'd made up her mind.

In a way, although it was nothing
to do with me really
I had 'helped' unknowingly.

At the gates she took my empty bottle
and gave me a small kiss.

Unsure of myself I walked back
to the car thinking of how ordinary
it felt to be kissed by a nun.

NIGHT HEAT

rain cracks sky
violently sparking black heaven
abrupt noise
globules spatting
drought-hardened earth
depetalising flowers

from my hot room
wearing just bare feet
and shorts
I enter this downpour

rivulets wash my heat clean
thrash hair wet to head
sniff moisture
mouth open
taste the moonless clouds

ceasing gently
tension,
wounding the night as it broke
heals

halfway to repairment
upside-down bicycle
helps the trees
plop water musically
I nose-dive
a wet yellow rose

night still warm
by daybreak no-one will know
the rain was here
except the insane sane
with drip-covered skins

THE BURGLAR'S WIFE

Toe creep
the night stalked
the dark stealthy
with hiding places.

To practise constantly
easing upstairs
without a creak.
The trick of not
placing the feet
in the middle
but on the edge
of stair steps.

To only sense
the noise of the ear
traffic streaking light
across a boned body
the ache of a soft chair
witching calm seductively.

Pick the bedroom lock
careful not to arouse
the woman asleep there.

A clothes-covered
blue wicker chair
takes this weight
silently.

Watching her slow breath
the shadows sit and wait
to become partners
in a subtle death.

GOLDEN BROWN

I like gentle autumns
everything slowing
delaying
the final season
drifting to hibernation
eking on the edge
of winter's death.

It started hot
but within days
      it rained.

      Purring on the pavements
      cycling through slush
      wrapped in waterproofing
      that's always
      just too hot
      or
      not hot enough.

         Worse was the wind
         pouring from the cracks
         of windows and doors
         blanketing you in cold.

Hot soups and broths
leeks for lamb stew
put fire inside until
the weather broke
and yellowing sunsets
threw horizoned light
to graze your ceiling.

Loving became more delicate
souls encountered lustfully

the bed gently warmed
no more summer's sweaty inferno
and not quite yet
the multi-blanketed haven
for your frosty toes.

We arrived at
the best season
          our autumn.

AT WORK: FEBRUARY

Humping and grumping
a six-hundred gallon
metal oil tank
on planks and rollers.

Heaving and wheezing
four men still
couldn't pick it up
a right bunch of Leonardos.

> I look into
> the dead eye
> of a gutted
> rabbit
> one of five
> in a row
> on a bamboo pole
> hung in a garage.

> Sully Isle
> tide up
> sunny winter wind
> spritening up the day
> working too hard
> to get cold.

Only two of us
yesterday
levering
sliding
grappling
it off the lorry
that couldn't get into
the narrow drive
and thirty yards

to the six-foot wall
we had to get it over.

    Old tank out
    new tank in.

When that was done
we painted it
in the sun
easy work
really.

AND NOW IT'S SUNDAY

Our conversation last night
your reluctance to tell
a revelation of your character.

Now told I have to re-adjust
your light particles
are a different colour
the transformation
of your every look
something to be guessed at.

Grey outlines surround us
tree bare except for lichen
Flat Holme, Steep Holme
long stone ridges jut
across the curved beach
a behemoth's rib cage
Lavernock Point
its dark lolling head.

Overgrown path
to an old ruined house
we stumble around
view and site are perfect
we imagine its former glory
older than you or I
a wealthy hide-away
or a well worked for home
"I could live here forever."

The rabbits have been around
all around
it's hard to place our feet
on clean grass.

January ears and noses
hair wind-flung back
pale faces, an icy wet kiss
the precursor of chapped lips.

This new you has stunned me
voiceless emotions
are unacceptable
wanting more you are peeved
at my inability to express
my delight, my amazement
and my uncertainty.

Anything but boring
I'm constantly surprised
at being wrong-footed
at feeling one step behind.

Walking the narrow road
a rusting sign says
'Swanbridge'
in black and white
the cold cutting through
the drifts of our coats
Sully Isle sleeps
in a bleak dull sea.

I point out two gulls
laying on the wind
you jokingly mistake them
for vultures
and you a 'country girl'.

Moving off the road
for a passing car
I fail three times
to throw pebbles

far enough
to cause a splash
in the ever-moving sea.

THIS CHILD HAS NO NAME

cold, hard, quick to the morning
hot tickings of metal cooling
she screams, but not with pain
their link breaking, songing hurt

and the fingers crawl out
placing themselves on heart
armfuls of joy and wet passion
calming that slow beast death

the seams of her life flow
hole in a boat of crying
covering the gape, the rend
persisting to be, make good

he shivers, but she feels not death
only cold hands taking him away
and the tears consume her face
welling her voice into grief

AT THE FUNFAIR

The place I wasn't
is where she was
strolling around
a closed funfair.

She told me about it
but I wasn't there either
before I put the phone down
her sad voice, "Goodbye".

Three days later she was
splurged across all
the front pages
"GIRL SLAIN IN FLAT".
All weekend she laid there
while I'd got angry
because she wouldn't
answer her phone.

I burnt the papers
tried not to remember
but I kept seeing her
at the funfair without me.

Even when they caught him
no-one had been to see me
didn't know I existed
I hadn't bothered
grief sealing me up.

'Unintentional'
'Mentally unstable'
so he only got five years
though he'd raped her first.

Nights wake me
from closed funfairs
a phobia of knives
stabbing at my chest
breathe in
breathe out
slowly like forgetfulness
I let the tears flow.
Never again will
I go to a funfair
without her.

BLATANT

Coming out of the dole office after an interview to see how I was getting on (patronizing bastards), I see them. They are on a large square of grass outside the Xerox shop at the junction of Wood St. and Westgate St. This dumb square of grass, I guess, is supposed to bring a little countryside to the city. Still, they like it; sitting, laying, rolling, spitting. Some are skinheads, swastikas, NF and proud of it. Who cares? Most are just nice boys, the sort you see in kids' programmes on the telly. Sun's out for a change and they're here, sucking up the toxic. Plastic bags billowing with their breath. The funny-for-no-reason smiles. Laugh. Go on laugh, it might be one of yours, anybodies. Who cares? And they're so blatant about it. Mind you it's not illegal, you can't ban glue can you? They can't drink alcohol so they've got to do something. Inhale it, snort it, sniff it. 'Bostik nostril' as the great MacSweeney put it. Make their, your, our world just go away. Everyone does that, it's just that for them the ways and means are limited. I walk past. So do you. What is anyone supposed to do? Who cares? If they want brain damage they can have it. Life in Thatcher's paradise might be more bearable with brain damage! One of them falls over. Laughs. You know, that can't-stop-it laugh. Fun! Who cares? Wonder how many trips you can get out of a tube or a tin of glue? Would it be comparable to other drugs such as booze? They go crazy sometimes, don't know what they're doing, attack people even! But that's rare, mostly it's just themselves they do in. Know what I mean? Who cares? I catch a bus. No I don't, I walk. It's a nice day. Save the money. You always need that little bit more than you've got when you're on the dole. Something. Always something you've got to buy. Some glue maybe? Who cares?

THE FAT UNDERBELLY

Cowboy developers riding high
the capital, quango, gravy train
selling themselves all ways and back
fast buck screwing us and the city.

Selling off the best buildings
gutted for plastic refurbishment
mutated leisure centres, shopping malls
not a good pub in choking distance.

Satisfied with 'making do'
contented by a successful greasing
by encroaching the poor's territory
with slicker cars, sharper hairstyles.

Their damp seeps into everything.
Poets bitch for arts council fobbings
begging the only art form increasing
and poverty our biggest employer.

Contractors are paid with our children
who can't afford to be unhealthy
who move to holes in Hirwaun and Ponty
because of the property baron's squeeze.

Separated from our reality by clout
insulated by safe retirement elsewhere
these headmen shit on our doorsteps
then leave believing we're grateful.

IS LOVE REAL?

1. Re-wiring

She told me she wanted
electro-convulsive therapy
because sometimes they wipe
whole sections of memory
times, places, people.
She wanted electric shocks
so maybe, just maybe
it would wipe him out.
She is crying again.
"Anything is better than this."

That's love I thought
remembered my own case
hadn't I tried to wipe her out
hopelessly trying to lose it
too painful to forget.

Looking at this women
she is in pain
visible pain
love.

2. "Do you think grand passions
     are just sex?" he asked.

"He was back
we were together again
hugging, kissing
I could feel his shirt
his arms around me
see him so clearly
vividly study his face.
It was rapturous

wonderfully real
I could smell him
taste his salty skin
all so perfectly.
When I woke up
I was already crying."

Even in her sleep
she knew.

LAUREATE

Sitting behind Big Hughey
I become intimate
with the back of his neck.

It is not at all hairy
smooth skin slides up
from shirt collar to hairline.

Just to the rear of the angular jawbones
underneath the wide ears
a few grey whiskers lurk

where maybe his razor
had unusually missed
or has he had plastic surgery?

When he gets up to read
he drags his poems out from hiding
in a small crumpled black bag.

He stands
like a sentinel
at the gates of doom.

His encapsulation of strangulation
mangulation and decapitation
render his audience nauseous.

After serious heavy metal
he cheers up to become
merely 'funereal'.

At the end
he shakes hands rapidly
and departs quickly.

This well-known exit of his
rumours him to be eccentric
but it's only too understandable

who could listen to, let alone read
an hour of intense, closed-in poetry
and not need to escape.

Walking into the deathly night
he achieves a brief moment
a monument to personal silence.

Outside he soon breathes easier
so when his audience happen upon him
he chats and signs books in the rain.

Surely if Superman were an eagle
he would have a profile
like Ted Hughes.

THE GREAT RASTAFARI ANGLO-WELSH SHEEP POEM

Dis likkle baaa laam
ees gowing tuh dee illside
runnin liek a crazee dred
tryin tuh git owtta dat poems rowd
but no ways yuh know
im lok up liek im was in Belsen
dee baarbs o dem daam poets
is goin tuh flees im backsied.

Waapnin tuh de poor sheeps
dem causing no aarm
is baad ways yuh baaldifies dem
aan meks dayuh natty wool
in tuh dem terribul bobbul jumpuhs
waat dee aanglow-wellsh edituhs wayuh
is baad ways yuh bertyuhs dem
puts dem on dee tabel aan den
meks owt daiz frum 'Selaand Newydd'.

Aan aas if daat int orl eenuf
is baad ways dem daam poets
riets dem daam poims abowt dee poer sheeps
on dee evun poeruh slaag eeps
aan orl dem daam poets
is filld up wid dee vegeteriunisum
mekin redundunt dee muttun aan laam
mekin dee sheeps evun poeruh
daan waat de daam poets is!

Maaaaan, aan waas dis?
Aanudder daam sheep poim!
klutturin up dee fleesee dred loks!
Waat I is waantin tuh see

65

is orl dem daapee sheeps
bleetin baak dayuh owen raantins
doowin sum wikid werdaydj
tuh dee daaam aanglow-wellshees
nort uh won uh dem blud klaart poets
got eenuf gumshun tuh bietee
dee bolloks offa baaa laaam!
        T......chuh!

PUTTING IT POLITELY
for Peter Finch

When he walked in we knew something would happen. A short man with the makings of a beard, dull clothes, proper boots and a grimy tanned face. He was carrying a sheep. He ignored the queue and walked right up to the counter. As he walked past you could smell him: smoky, acrid and something else too, something warm and animal. He looked straight at the man behind the counter who was filling in a form. We could taste the tension.

Finally the man looked up, not really a man just a kid with spots, younger than I was, some school leaver with one O-level too many. He seemed embarrassed by the man and looked around before speaking. "I'm afraid you'll have to wait in the queue." "FUCK YOU AND YOUR FUCKING QUEUE!" The man threw the sheep over the counter at the boy who was stupid enough to catch it. The weight of it, kicking and frantic, hit hard and his chair toppled backwards. The sheep baaaa'd loudly. "THAT'S WHAT I THINK OF YOU, YOU BASTARDS. I HAVEN'T HAD A CHEQUE IN MONTHS! I'M ILL ON THE SICK AND MY SHEEP ARE DYING AND WHAT DO YOU DO ABOUT IT? FUCKING FUCK ALL THAT'S WHAT! I PAY MY TAXES AND MY NATIONAL INSURANCE. I KNOW WHAT I'M ENTITLED TO. JUST CAUSE I LIVE OUT IN THE COUNTRY YOU THINK YOU CAN FUCKING IGNORE ME, WELL YOU FUCKING WELL CAN'T!"

The boy had struggled to his feet and was shouting for security. "FUCK SECURITY YOU BASTARD, WHAT ABOUT MY FUCKING MONEY?" A big dollopy looking man in a tight-fitting dark blue uniform came out of the side door. "Come on now, we can't be having this now can we?" "OH WE FUCKING CAN'T EH!" "Now look you, you just behave yourself. If you can't be civil then you'll have to leave." And he put his hand on the little man's arm. "FUCKING GERROFF! I'LL GO WHEN I'VE FUCKING WELL HAD MY MONEY." His defiance was thrilling to us. Security pointed his thick finger at him menacingly. "Now look you, you leave now or believe me you'll be sorry." Someone at the back shouted, "Leave him alone yuh big bully", and then we were all off, "He only wants his money." "Yeah, let him alone." "Yuh big fascist pig!" As usual there were a lot of us in the queue and we were all on the little man's side. Security looked around nervously. "Right then," he said, "if that's your attitude, we'll get the police and let them sort it out." And he stomped back through the side door. "Better get out of it quick mate," someone said "you'll get no joy here." The little man jumped the counter, grabbed the sheep and clambered back over with it. "FUCK EM ALL!" he said as he went out, "THEY'RE ALL FUCKING BASTARDS!" And we all cheered.

Moments later the police arrived but, fortunately enough, he was long gone. They looked around and talked to security but didn't bother with us. We just shuffled quietly forward, like sheep into a pen. Not long after this incident the grids went up and then, eventually, the plastic windows were fitted.

THE HOOK
for Duncan Bush

At 6.30 a.m.
pallets are being
unloaded by crane.

We wait
as the boxes
of Scandinavian butter
            descend toward us.

The wind races along
the dockside
        through us
            and into
                the city.

Our load is welcomed
    gently to earth
            by many hands.

A metal ball
pivoted to counterweight
the hook
automatically releases
four looped ropes.

I recognise
from his drawings
Leonardo's design
so simply perfect
five hundred years on
no-one has bettered it.

The dockers 'handball'
the butter onto our lorry

each box counted
        accounted for.

Rain spits at us
as we haul tarpaulin
slipping it over
        tying it down
using that particular knot
        and rope pattern
I now do easily.

After one more hard week
this job will finish
I'll be back on the dole
getting up at mid-day.

The hook
not now in use
but confident
    of its future
            sways
                flecking
        the rain.

THE BICYCLE IS AN EASY PANCAKE

traffic dazzles
metal thronging
whizzing whirring
engines roaring
blood frenzying
   screeches
  dodges
 swerves
gutter dives
a wobbling concoction
on two wheels
trying to get
   what the!
out the way of
that huge lorry
"FUCKING LORRIES!"
a near catastrophic
   attempt
to accelerate
faster than a Volvo
"FUCKING VOLVOS!"
honks & beeps
shouts & jeers
obscene gesticulations
from & at
drivers behind windscreens
engines farting
exhaust fumes in my face
taking chances across lights
that never work slow enough
    for bicycles
another lorry driver
  who can't see what
  the arse end of his

vehicle is doing
swaying into my
beejobbuld
unbalanced
leaping
off the bike
& dragging it
onto the pavement
so it & I don't get crushed
by a 23-ton
cargo cubicle
from Guyana
FANCY BEING KILLED
FOR THE SAKE OF
SOME FUCKING
BANANAS!
rhythm, pace, movement
a combination of every sense
to help me survive
this chaotic madhouse
called traffic
drivers joking
teaching me what's what
swerving in & scaring me

they think I shouldn't be
in the middle of the street
I'm waiting to turn right
that's all I want to do
get around a corner
into a side road
but still they come at me
horns blaring
headlights flashing
"What's that fucking idiot
doing on that bike?

I'll teach him to be out there
where he shouldn't be."
"I'm on my side
of the white line
YOU PRICK!"
luckily for me he misses
and I'm off the main street
my tyres roll onto
newly laid tarmac
a smoothness
so sweet
I can hardly feel
the bike beneath me
the road climbs up
into a long
hard
steep hill
the other side of which
the countryside waits
my rhythmic pedalling slows
pushing the pedals down
to go up
heaving & pedalling
pushing & pulling
I stand up out of the saddle
my full weight forcing down
pedal & heave
heave & pedal
the heat beginning to tell
pulling on the handlebars
hands sweaty
on slippery wet metal
heave & pedal
the motion
pedal & heave
the slogging rhythm

heave & pedal
tyres melting into the road
road melting into the tyres
heaving my way uphill
through an ocean of treacle
pushing down on the pedals
pulling up on the handlebars
the heaving rhythm
the aching motion
again & again & again
breathing the fiery hot air
down into my lungs
heave & pedal
pedal & heave
pushing to the top
fighting through
humid gravity
dense & clammy
heave & pedal
pedal & heave
gnats sticking
to hot red wet skin
sweat running off me
heave & heave & heave
legs straining with hurt
but I keep on reaching
until I see the sun
rise up over the summit
finally
agonizingly
I'm there
pedalling becomes easier
easy
at the crest
I sit back
overheated

                                   my bike trickles along
                                                quietly
                                                slowly
                                             it floats
                                        over the edge
                                       glides downhill
                                       speeding down
                                      faster & faster
                                    hands come free
                                  off the handlebars
                                 stretch out horizontal
                                        like wings
                              capturing the still air
                                 blowing past me
                              evaporating my sweat
                                 filling hair
                          eyes, ears, nose, mouth
                           & lungs with coolness
                          I'm freely flying
                         swooping around
                       winding country bends
                       handlebars start vibrating
                       with the increasing speed
                                      I grip them
                     stones sniker-snak out
                        from under tyres
                     greenery blurring past me
                     beauty, freedom, freshness
                        slung in my face
                     the speed
                        magnificent
                     the smell of manure
                        magnificent
                     I swing out off the hill
                  hitting a stretch of road
                     long & flat

I've cooled off completely
I can feel goose-bumps
I start the rhythm going
pedalling
      pushing
            rhythming
hitting my stride
heaving down on pedals
rubber beating the road
sprockets
cogs
ball bearings
rotating
revolving
gears sliding
in & out
chain leaping
up & down
metal teeth
pulling
heaving
hubs
rims
tubes
tyres
wheeling around
flashing spokes
into invisibility
knees pistoning
cranks whirling
a travelling machine
in perfection
pedal & rhythm
rhythm & pedal
I'm still not hot
my bike speed

knocking my heat away
pedal & rhythm
rhythm & pedal
heart beating
legs pumping
arms pulling
my whole body
working the magic
the force
the pedal
the rhythm
the circle
around around
up down
down up
pushing
pulling
wheels
spinning
speeding
arcing corners
leaning over
knees out
like Barry Sheene
hugging the side
allowing cars to pass
drivers in hot sweaty seats
me out here in the air
     alive
feeling everything
tingling vitality
pumping & pedalling
pedalling & pumping
& the rhythm
& the cycle
& life

rhythm & cycle
again & again & again
around a bend I hark
& there in the distance
is a red light
signalling me to halt
I cease pedalling
back pedal a few times
ratcheting
ease on the brakes
feel the bike shudder
as they bite
decelerating
till the front wheel just rolls
over the white line before
it stops with a final jerk
of my fingers
I wait for the bike
to slightly fall
sideways
before I put my foot down
I flick the gnats & flies
off shirt & skin
as I've stopped
the air has stopped
rushing past me
allowing my heat
to catch up
   I listen to the hum
      of life
        raise my head
          look at the hazy sun
                  its warmth
          beating down on me
        my heart beating my blood
         around my veins

my tired & weary
aching legs & arms
                beating me
            I sit there
        feeling beaten
                        but alive
                        & I listen
                        & listen
                        & listen
                    to the feeling
                            of summer
                    & it comes to me
                        with a buzz
                            in my ears

                ssssshshshseeeeeiit!
                                do
                                I
                                love
                                cycling

ANGIN ABOWT

ROYAL WEDDING

In his shorts, whistled at and ogled by the secretaries
his job had been to hang the reams of bunting
criss-crossing the sleek, glass skyscraper's front
ready to celebrate the newly-weds' royal procession.

On the big day he smuggled his girlfriend to the roof where
opposite a gull's nest, near the maniacal window-cleaner's lift
with her leant over the edge, as she liked, they fucked
as the crowds waved and the gull wheeled and divebombed.

After being on the top of every multi-storey carpark
this was the best, the highest and the mad gull
flapping and raucous, added to the excitement.
How could they climb further up than Churchill House?

Mountains weren't the same, even on ledges or cliffs
they were too isolated, not enough risk of being caught.
She loved the thought of people surrounding her but
below and not seeing, that and the exhilarating height.

His roofing job had them up three church spires
sacrilegiously thrilling as was the dodging security
in the trade union centre on Cathedral Road
one up for the workers in a heady downpour.

Shagged out they shout at the cheering throng below
and she hurls her knickers like a demented Tom Jones fan.
They sail away, as if it's the end of something, to finally settle
on the aerial of the Prince and Princess's black limousine.

BUYING SHARES IN THE JOBCENTRE

I been ovuhdrawn now fuh almost for yers
an no way uh payin it off liek.
Des always dat unakownted bil, yewno
dee gas, lectric or me onlee luksuree, duh fown.
I carn fink ow jus livin
kun so eeklips me inkum liek
I doan smowk or drink uh loh
an no waze um I uh bludee fashun viktim
an as fuh eggsortik fuwds liek
yew no, I aven bort uh stayk
in wel ovuh uh yer now!
Bakun offkuts, dass me onlee reggewla meet
nor frew tyoiss miend buh eekonomiks.
Wah wif dee impropuh dieyat
an naf orl entuhtaynment
(evun seks iz kostlee)
les fayss it, lief's aardlee wurf livin izit?
Ger uh job dey sez, urn uh few bob
buh jeezus ders no wurk iz zeh?
Pettee kryim, fiduls, evun a weeks onnest
o yeh, orl uh dart, buh nor reel wurk liek
fullee payeed, taksd an inshored an nat
yoo's godda bee kidin!
Duh blak maarkits dee ownlee fing
dass keepin Fatyurz paradice gowin init!
If ownlee I new wear ir wuz gowin?
Orl I noes fuh shor iz
iss nor gowin mi bludee way izit?

LINES AT LLANTWIT MAJOR
i.m. John Tripp

Coming across the cliff-top path
I cross a stone stile
it's bar polished to a shine
many times daily
by little kiddie's knees
the flounced buttocks
of overweight ramblers
and the sweaty crotches
of the less than agile.

Whetstone smooth it will glisten
buffed for centuries
till the too young, the too old
and the far too heavy
wear it all down.

At the excuse for a beach
a motley gathering
of rocks, pebbles and sewerage
the fishers bait their hooks
and cast towards an England
far too close for comfort.
I could swim to it
and maybe I will
but not today
and not from here.

I spread my packet jam
on my overcooked scone
sip tea from a cup which
doesn't match or fit its saucer
and sit viewlessly facing
a pretend old stone wall
speckled with yellow.

If this car-park-by-the-sea
is Llantwit Major
what can possibly be
on offer at Llantwit
or even Llantwit Minor?

CONTACT

Near steamed up windows
the bar is cloudy with conversation
as I try and tell the jokiness
about what it's like being poor
the worries, the unpayable bills etc.
"Christ we all get them you know!"
"Yes but you can afford them."
Suddenly I'm being lectured;
"Middle-class debt, you've no idea boy!
My mortgage is crucifying me
and the cost of kids, well jesus
it's enough to make you want to give up sex!"
They all laugh and so do I.
He's got a two hundred thousand pound house
two cars, lodgers, a working wife
and a job earning more in one year
than I'd get in ten years on the dole.
They tell me to 'stop moaning'
so I do, of course, mates don't want berating.
"Come to think of it, it's your round isn't it?"
So at the bar, amidst their empties, I order
and as the till rings, I count my money.

CONFESSIONS OF A BABYSITTER
for Marilyn

1.

Babies are the easiest, so they say.
Always at the film's climax, the crying
and you wander up strange stairs
to a dark room, mouthing consolation.
Sometimes it's enough just to be there
but when they're teething you have to give
rocking them, singing those old lullabies
trying to remember when you heard them last
softly, deeply, imitating the heart's beat
"There there, there there, there there…"
It rarely fails to quiet them
sending them back to their mother womb
the safest place any of us have ever been.

2.

That movement outside the door's open crack
noticed through the flickering television's light.
Open it and, sleepy eyed, there she is
snivelling, mouth puckered, jerkily sobbing
"I can't sleep" "I'm thirsty" "My leg's hurting"
or the one that always makes me work
"Mummeee, I want my mummeee, where is sheee?"
"Just popped over the shop that's all
she'll be back any minute now."
The whining subsides.
Get her a drink or dip the dummy in honey
turn the TV down, hum a bit, hope it works.
Every creaking stair stirs her.
In her room I see the problem
the bulb has gone on her Minnie Mouse lamp.
I draw the curtains, let in the orange street light

to scatter her fears and nightmares.
Every other move I make she wakes.
Laying her on the bed I lay with her
till she's asleep and then spend forever
trying to extract my arm from under her.
It is more asleep than she is
a dead weight to be gently tugged at.
Closing the door not quite shut
I step onto the landing and relax
to hear, "Mummeee!"

3.

Who would be an uncle?
Joanne, the eldest, is wailing grizzles
on the floor, legs kicking, screaming.
"Go on scream, scream all you want."
So she does, louder, even more raucous.
"Your mother will be here in a minute."
Desperately trying to convince her and myself
as if hope could make my sister appear.
I get angry, yell at her
but I know it won't work, never does.
Gentleness is what will calm and cajole her
either that or bribery (oh for chocolate
or that last extra television programme
they're not supposed to watch).
James is jumping, trampolining on the settee.
Action Man, He-Man and the Incredible Hulk
all rolled into one small Terrar
and he can't even speak yet!
Alison, like myself, is the middle child
they're always the most well adjusted
having someone older to learn from
and someone younger to blame their mistakes on.
She has, by now, gone to bed of her own accord
neatly fed up with the other's antics.

By the time my sister gets home
they'll be tucked up in beddy-byes
sleeping logs in the land of nod.
"Were they good?" And I'll smile sheepishly
"Good as gold, no problem at all."

THROTTLE

The man unexpectedly left us with him
in the small bland room, coffin lid removed.
My father said; "Poor bugger." almost crying.
I was surprised to see he was so upset
I was too young at twenty-three
to fully grasp that it was Gramp
though it obviously was I could see
those hands, at ninety-four, so delicate
bruises blossomed at a touch.
My father's staunchness wavering
as we stared down into morbidity
laid out and swathed in red satin.

I recall that time he couldn't sleep
so I'd come down, lifted him, lit a cigarette.
As he smoked I asked him what
was the happiest time he could remember?
He inhaled. He exhaled. Scanned ninety-four years.
"The strike in the twenties during the summer.
We'd go in to see if there was any work
and then we'd be off, down the beach
or over to Weston or up the Brecons on motorbikes."
I'd seen pictures, small, dapper, watch chain
straw boater and the motorbike he built himself.
I thought of sunshine, a country lane
a motorbike throttle being twisted.

My father hung on till time seemed enough
then, with relief, went to talk to the funeral director.
I took one last glance at those hands
mottled purple by gentleness.

WATER

'And whoever moves away is still held back
by miraculous water.'
          Vernon Watkins 'The Broken Sea'

Sat in the kitchen he told us
"Marvellous properties water y'know
I see em at the ospital
can't move an eyelid
but as soon as they're in water
they're paddlin round
moving like seals."

As he spoke
the old woman upstairs
watched turgid afternoon TV
'The Love Boat'
floating her life away.

A large wooden house
full of first-edition books
Louis Stevenson, Walter Scott
and Hemingway. Antiques litter.
Paintings, all done by the 'master'
who had travelled and was long dead
testified to art as a hobby.
The second-rate Turners and Monets
are all of the sea, lakes, ponds, pools
and, occasionally, rain.

Sun on our backs, our shovels cutting
a long narrow trench three feet deep
to lay a plastic pipe connecting
the mains supply to their first tap
bringing water, the so-called life force.

She'd been the maid and could now live
in this house until she died
which wouldn't be too far off.
The man just came to look after her.

His laughter spiced our tea
"Used to piss in our boots years ago
when we wuz ploughin the fields
piss in our boots, aye!
It wuz the alkalies in it
soothed yur blisters
marvellous thing water."

HILL END, LLANGENNITH

The sea and dunes are shrouded
surrounded by thick fog.
Running barefoot, full pelt
across the visual wilderness
sand below and all above
smothering damp grey blindness.

Saltiness clouding his face
his speed bringing elation
he pounds up the dune's
steep sand-slip avalanche
thigh muscles tightening
with an ache of breathlessness.
Lungs gasp at the sparse grass summit
with visibility nil he can only survey
his surfer's beach-bum feelings.
He was born for sea and sand's caress.

In the car, out of the fleecy rain
preparing for the long drive back
he watches the surf widows
sat in their boyfriend's
chunky four-wheel drives
reading, chatting, chewing apples
waiting for the surf to go down
their men to come home.

Just before he was due to leave
a couple come back and he waits
watches the girl peel off her wetsuit
with a deliciously erotic difficulty.
Memories curl over him of when
year after suntanned year they came
surfed till they were blue from the cold

how as a child he'd sat on that wall
and decided to be a writer.

He was amazed that this pilgrimage
the first in fifteen years
should be rewarded by so little
in the people and place having changed.
The seagulls noisily surf the atmosphere
as his Maxi, its clutch slipping badly
bumps up the old track's deep ruts.
He is thinking of a wetsuit.

SCAFFOLDING

I love the way scaffolding goes up
with only one spanner, like adult Meccano.
Ely boys barking insults and laughing
as they swing various sized poles
to lift and then swing again
before being laid or slotted.
Clamps are thrown about like monkeys
flying around trees, playing catch.
Pikon'd to the building, all movement
becomes solid and the scaffolders
brachiate down, to leave it,
a climbing frame for work.

Later, looking across the old guano'd slates,
I move aside to let someone pass
and, as I lean on the end crosspole,
the whole thing comes away in my hand.
Everyone laughs as I fail to fall.

ABOVE US ONLY

Sky
you don't notice it at ground level
but when you're on a roof
as on a mountain or at sea
you are surrounded by it
the mass that brings weather.

There you learn to read it
the cloud over the sun
cooling for hot heavy work
like bumping slates and such
become intimate with different rains
that which you can work in
spitting to steady drizzle
to the darkly thunderous cloud
looming across the great map
every glance a blip
like a satellite sequence
in between the hammer's falling
till it stops work and moves you
swinging down at the last minute
to hide under scaffolding planks
as rain sizzles on every surface
plummets from unfinished gutter ends.

After a cigarette and mundane conversation
it stops and between plops
you can feel the silence of the air.

Hauling yourself up over rust wet iron
to place one buttock in the seeping damp
breath will be crisper, light brighter
slates and nails slippery and inevitably
as movement occurs unexpectedly
the hammer will hit the cold finger

and a curse will be swallowed up
by that immense atmosphere
sky.

18th SEPTEMBER

Sun
relentlessly pouring fire
liquids oozing from skin
energy rapidly depleting
wavering the balance
felt rolls and slips
falling.

Slates
too hot to handle
fondled delicately
groped quickly into position
their heat sweating legs
bared in shorts
knees red and indented
bruised.

Dust
sticking to skin
leaving black lines
along material's every fold
demarcating where shoe meets sock
rubs itself into eyes
blurring.

Dinnertime
tea and eggs
scotched of course, pork pies
cheese and ham rolls
saliva dripping bacon butties
cream cake and iced bun
enough to leave any fat
burping.

Cramp
the ache of a ladder
rough batten wood
seethes across skin
crouched joints cracking
pins and needles eased into
stretched.

Stinging
soaps into cuts
bits itching body angles
the digital metal watch removed
duplicated by sweat moulded dirt
round base and every strap link
a negative's white
skeleton.

BLACK SUNDAY

All day on the roof
8 in the morning till 8 at night
sweat caking the slate dust
like miners before their bath
thick fuzzy hungover heads
aching we bumped slates.

Walking across the battens
my foot slipped, went through the felt
banged my dodgy knee
the one that, occasionally, gives out
as it did then while I wrestled
a pile of slates on the slide.

I watched the tape
thrown up from the ground
bounce off the bedroom window pane
to leave a frenzied web of cracks.

Orange dye from the string line
twanged straight for the battens
passed its marks onto everything.

Slate hammers low slung like holsters
we should have been on horses
rustling cattle, robbing banks
not up on a roof
acting as if we knew
what we were doing.

With the battens on the final roof
we'd bumped the rest of the slates
carried them on sunburnt shoulders
shirts sashed for pads Sinbad style.

While the others had a smoke
drawing it out, being paid by the day
I'd wanted to get it done, out of the way
and so toiled on for a little while
a lot of sweat and too much weariness
till I'd also had to take it easy.

It was, after all, Sunday
a day of rest, religion doesn't count
everyone needs time to catch their breath.

OCTOBER 1987

Windflap coruscating balance
unwieldy, unrolled, yard-wide felt
wrestling its resistance into place
through a storm of swear words
till it's battered down with battens
and hammered galvanized slate nails.
Persistence gradually covering up
the grim gusting gale swept roof
held by the batten's wide ladder
reaches the crest's cutting edge
a cold punch in the face
the rip slices ears, shears wet eyes
lashes hair and bedraggles hats
blues hands, billows us off balance
as unnerving as roofing can get.

With only one side finished so are we
clamber carefully down, tool laden
around the large wet grey rectangle
of asbestos slates left for tomorrow
to morning warm us, bumping them
up to lay stacked like fallen dominoes.
Into the old, dirty, rocking van
and head for home and evening meals
a hell of a day gratefully done.

Later, as food is hungrily consumed
television tells us of the hurricane
the fifteen million trees blown down
the footage of a roof torn off
slates rippling, then splattered upwards.
We sit remembering how we'd joked
"A bit windy today init?"
laughing now as if we'd known
but because we hadn't.

TYNDALL STREET

Staggering under new rolls of felt
up glass besmattered staircases
three floors and then the ladder
to the stiff trap door for the roof
which is surrounded by a small wall
three foot high, eighteen inches thick.

You could've walked in the lead gully
peering over the wall but the thieves
ripped it all up, sold it for scrap
probably not worth the work
but needed all the same by men
with families to feed and no jobs.

After three morose trips up and down
the roofing felt is heavier than lead
at the final fixed ladder to the sky
and then there are the asbestos slates
odd bits of wood, nails, roof battens
and the worn bag of tools to fetch.

Mooching around the second floor
there's a huge flywheel suspended
on its heavy bar close to the ceiling.
Motor and band sold off long ago
the heart of this building powering
lathes or looms in the last century.

As work goes on we look across
from Bute East Dock to Tiger Bay
all derelict ground stained black
lumpen wooden and iron machines
rusting, dented, left at odd angles
a mortuary for forgotten industry.

Empty buildings, brickwork cracked
rooves holed, windows smashed
scarred and potholed dead-end roads
waiting for time's wrecking ball
to flatten this outdated wasteland
so a future can smother these ghosts.

It's hard to believe that this was once
a mass of ships loading and unloading
warehouses filling and emptying
cranes swinging, lorries transporting
men enthralled by endless hard labour
when our history was thrumming.

We hurl broken slates into the dock
across a morass of oil-soaked disuse
someone is paying to repair this roof
to put cheap felt where the lead was
patch the holes, hold back the rain
for this building marked for saving.

After a few long grey days we finish
take a last look at Cardiff's arsehole
this squalid nadir end of the line for coal
then carry the tools slovenly back down
to the old Morris van, lock up and leave
the past glowering in the urban twilight.

ANGIN ABOWT

ees up there
makin the roof
'more betterer' (ee laughs)
I'm down ere
catchin raindrops
gobbin on earwigs
watchin em curl up
that ole cement bucket
risin on the orange rope
to im up there
doin I doan know what
the flashin on the chimney
nailin the odd slate on
searchin for the screwdriver
what ee's been sat on an then
avin to go back up
the moved ladder to get it

sat on the wall
under the tree
backs to the hedge
well out of the rain
ee passes me a Welsh mint
as the late lunches
come out of The Beverley
the pavement all dug up
traffic jammin
that lorry flattenin those bollards
we laugh at the navvies
swearin at the clerks
behind their thin backs
especially one dozy lookin git
in a yellow plastic mac

"ees a university tyke
 knows bugger all about it I'll bet
 tryin to teach em their job, christ!
 dey knows more than ee'll ever know"
"aye" I replies, lookin at
 that sore dark spot
 where I jammed my thumb
 between two sections of gutterin
 to rediscover the agony
 an the racism
 of a 'black man's pinch'

 ee gets up to go back on top
 it's not really rainin now
 an my thumb's stopped throbbin
 ee looks at me, smiles
"university!
 dat's where dey
 takes yuh brains out yur ead
 an shoves em up yur arse init?"

A CRISIS OF CONSCIENCE IN THE VOTING BOOTH

His hand hovers
wavering indecisiveness.
Hypothermia clutched his father
a life-long Tory till death,
but what now?
Could even he have wanted
a third term of Tory rule?

The muscles refuse to act
quivering for an X.
His son has eight O levels
three years on the dole
and prospects which do not exist
like the X in the blue's box.

A hardboard box
and makeshift with it.
What a place to decide
the future of British politics.
Poised strangely, facing wood
it reminds him of a coffin.

Such a small, stubby pencil
tied with string, obviously priceless.
Indented into its side; 'Made in Taiwan'.
"Bloody foreign crap!" his shout jabs
annoyance snaps the lead tip.

Viciously he scrapes his mark
slides pencil through the knot
snaps it and posts it
in the ballot box with the folded vote.
Later they will declare, 'null and void'
his, "BOLLOCKS!"

TAP DANCING IN THE SLAUGHTERHOUSE
for Ken Smith

All those headless bodies
blood, guts and nuclear weapons
hanging over our picked skulls
AIDS eating away at every carcass
eroding the world's excrement
soon to be a major portrayal
within the three-minute warning
of the latest party political broadcast
effluently molesting the TV screen
force feeding lies to an underfed nation
teaching us masturbation and flagellation
because if we beat ourselves
we've only ourselves to blame
and no one else's genitals get dirty.
The wrong name is unfortunate.
The wrong attitude is punishable.
The wrong income bracket
is about as shitty as you can get
but
your vote is still wanted.

ALAS POOR YORRICKS

To don a condom, or not to don a condom,
                    that is the question:
Whether 'tis safer to don a condom and suffer
The pins and needles of outrageous genital cramp,
Or to boldly enter, unsheath-ed, a sea of HIV positives,
And by copulation disperse them? – To spread – to carry:
Evermore; and, by this spread, thus we can end
The groin-ache, and the thousand unnatural perversions
That flesh is heir to, – 'tis a contamination
Recently to be fear'd. To lust,– to fuck; –
To fuck perchance to orgasm: – aye, there's the rub;
For in that fuck of fear what orgasms may
When we have struggled on that constrictive rubber
Which must give us pause: there's the relaxant
That makes a calamity of such good sex;
For who can bear the slips for prolonged time,
The strangled dong, the pangs of imprisoned love,
The lust's delay, the insolence of rubber,
And the giggles that await it from some unworthy types,
When he himself might his quietus make
With a bare bodkin?
For whom would fardels bare, and for how much?
The uncover-ed penis, of whose spawn
No reveller admits, rubbers now fill,
And makes us rather bonk those we have had,
Than bonk with others we know not of!
Thus AIDS doth make cowards of us all;
And thus the native hue of copulation
Is sick-lied o'er with the pale cast of sheath;
And enterprises of great lust and excit-e-ment,
With this regard, their moments turn awry,
And lose the name of PASSION!

SOMETHING'S AWRY

NEVER IN ADLESTROP
With a nod to E.T. and D.A.

No. Not Adlestrop, nor Winkleigh, Bude
or Husbands Bosworth – besides the name
hardly matters. Nor did I languish in June heat.
Simple, I stood too early on the empty platform
and the wrong train came in slowly.
It stopped the wrong side of the tracks
next to the other platform. From a window
a very, very pretty girl leaned out.

She smiled. I smiled. She waved. I waved.
She poked her tongue out. I pulled a funny face.
She laughed. I danced a jig, goose-stepped
and failed, chaotically, to do a cartwheel.
The train started to move out. I blew a kiss.
She lifted her T-shirt, flashed her bellybutton,
then disappeared into the carriage and out of my life.
I jumped off the platform, went clean over the rails,
hurled open the train door, leapt in and shouted;
"I love you!" to a pot-bellied man with a whippet.

Frantically I searched as the train gathered speed
then, glancing out the window, I saw her.
She, having alighted from the train,
was on the opposite platform, waiting.
As I was rapidly carried away, I knew not where,
I watched her fade to a distant speck
while the whippet surreptitiously sniffed my leg.

KIDNEYS

"That faint smell of urine."
  He dropped it into the conversation
  with such a casual Irish accent
  but it stood out for her
  not knowing it was a quote
  and she giggled and couldn't stop.
  That this man, one of Ireland's greatest
  should flex his literary muscles so
  only to have them withered
  by a girl's mocking laughter
  a thing too honest to be covered up.
"It was just so poetic!" She splurted
  over baked potatoes and quiche
  even the Romanian turned his head.
  I'm sure old James, rocking slowly
  one knee raised and clasped with both hands
  would have enjoyed the interplay
  which must have ended, but didn't
  when she explained to me
  the meaning of hirsute.

SOMETHING IN THE ARTS

She is off skiing
just for the weekend
mind
doesn't believe in
monogamy.
She's something
in the arts
restoration
rather than creativity.
She loves to drive her
open-top sports car
which doesn't always start.
The man she's in love with
isn't her steady boyfriend
they both believe in being
independent.
She is fair, tall and thin
her hair is slightly kinky
looks chic in a poor way
has an upper-class
north London accent.
The man she's in love with
doesn't know it
so she's going to have to
chase him a bit
and she doesn't know when
she can make it back to Cardiff
though she likes my poetry.

AUBURN

Fog bound up the motorway
to art, wine and sun in Swansea
and the girl I'm after is not after me
but it's okay because after
The Albert and Worthington Dark
it's Big Jake's party with Double Dragon
and Cassie, Cancer, 23
separated, sailor, Southampton
cheekbones, lips, blouse undone
auburn hair the colour
of my light-mauve slippers
dancing, drinking, partying
driving my old Maxi
down then up this city
full of hills and potholes
till we arrive by the ocean
stagger into her empty home
and straight to the bed
the bra strap
the condom
the groping, sweating
panting, positions, cramps
crumpled muscles, creased skin
mess wrecking the bed
glued to love's underbelly
swathing in orgasms
pulling up the bedclothes
sucking in the sleep
and drifting out to sea.

Waking early
Mumbles Head, slipper head
and what do you want for breakfast?
"Sex on toast is fine by me!"

BLUE

That first time we made love
you laughing apprehensively
as my light blue sheets tangled me
winter cold I was concerned
to keep the chill from our flesh.
Moments later you reached up
pulled the lights cord like a signal
and we became darkness.

As we warmed and writhed
the sheets fell from our love making
and my eyes grew accustomed
to the dim light from the living room
shining ever-so-faintly upon us.
Your body was sheathed in blue
I don't know where from or how
a deep, black blue, not quite luminous
all else being shadow.

Holding your head in my hands
the mixture of blue light and black shadow
changed every feature but for your eyes
staring back at me; I kissed them
as if you were some other woman
and in our naked electric I wondered
if I were blue for you.

AFTERWARD 2.25 A.M.

in the early hours
oh how many times
have I walked home
through empty streets
bathed in orange
entranced by the loneliness
inebriated by the pavement
the steady pace of scuffed souls
brushing past rough corners
around indomitable buildings
on the edge of teeth
the dry wet taste gulped
pressure of echoes on moist eyes
the coolness of night
hearing the trees
wind rustling the garbage
a leaf plucked from a hedge
this is the dream journey
homing pilot on automatic
nerve endings skinned by pleasure
oh how many times
in the early hours

DETAINED

opening my mouth
      words
    do not come out
         only a brief
     release of air
    from the lungs
but the words
    were to say
        so much
   now left
unsaid
   caught
    kept
permanently
  detained

translated
  what is said
       is
       "I love you"
but will you understand
or will you only hear
      just
       one
        small
         sigh!

SLIPPING

The two bananas
        you left me
        are looking out of place
        on my table
they are laid
        one on top of the other
            like exhausted lovers
                physically joined
                only at one point
                    but fitting all over
                    having grown together.

On the floor
        there is a small metal piece
            broken off
                my bed-settee.

SHE SAID IT
A poem for spring

"Have you been rolling around
         in flowers or something?"

Oh! Yes, that's just it
rolling around in flowers
all day long rolling
         flowers rolling
         rolling flowers
         me rolling flowers
         flowers rolling me
it's an occupation
         full-time employment
fit to cure all afflictions
         except maybe dizziness

Isn't it strange
         other people think so

I'm home now
         after a hard day's rolling
I listen to two girls gossiping
         outside my open door
I'd like to go and close it
         but after rolling in flowers
         it would be too obvious
         and I'd get embarrassed

That is what
         rolling around in flowers
                                   is

And laughter

LOVE POEM FOR JANET

Shut up Janet
Just shut up Janet
Janet shut up
Dammit Janet shut up
Shut up dammit Janet
Janet dammit
Will you shut up
Dammit Janet shut up
Oh kick the car Janet
Go on kick it dammit
That won't fix it
Janet
The car didn't get us lost
Dammit
You did
Janet
I can get lost on my own
Dammit
I don't need your help
Janet
Oh for god's sake shut it
Will you just
Shut it dammit Janet
Janet dammit shut it
shut it Janet dammit
Dammit Janet shut it
Dammit Janet
Where are you going
Janet
Dammit Janet
Where are you going?
Oh Dammit
One eency weency
Little bit
Of criticism
Janet
And you walked out
Dammit!

SOMETHING'S AWRY

1.

Among the wasps
getting slightly red
reading Basil's 'Odes'
dry grass upshooting
through red towel thread.

He reads of skin on skin
smiles with expectancy.

2.

Naked she
does not want to
diametrically opposed
they've got this far.
Eros spelled backwards
is sore.

3.

Black vinyl car seat
hotter than lust
he waits double parked
two wardens closing in.

In the house
she is on the phone
agreeing to a favour
for a man she doesn't like.

4.

They jibe heinous insults
laugh, knowing they're not meant
well, maybe not, uncertainty makes them
keeping away silences
parting on unknown thoughts
bad impressions festering.

5.

They make love
and love it
intercourse
does not occur
in its place
something more
intimate.

6.

Tiredness
unenjoyment
she 'goes off'
not speaking.

The pit of love
apathy incarnating.

7.

Heat moods
love to be shed
a tear unseen.

8.

Mere seconds in sex
can mean the world
but they managed
to come together
six days after
they'd 'split up'
for the first time.

9.

They talk.
Her; of ripping last pages
out of books he's yet to read.
Him; of making it with blond
Jane from the office.

They chide each other so
bantering love
as if they do not care.

10.

Sanctimoniously
indignantly
about their love
she repeatedly writes
terrible 'last poems'.

11.

Sitting in his car
rain hitting the roof
arguing with the darkness
knowing he's probably done
the wrong thing again
he drives off.

12.

Merthyr Mawr
sand rippling to the sea
wind flecking the dunes.
Tasting of salt
they make love
cold and gritty.

13.

Nothing to do but argue
blowing into each other's mouths
denying what they both know
feelings of entrapment
something is more than awry.

14.

She wraps herself
in cling film
hoping it will preserve
his excitement
and their love
but…

He discovers
in her transparent
heat sweating
sticky glistening
sheathed body
that holes
have to be made
to let her out
him in.

15.

They make love
just one more
'last time'.

It tastes of ending
sour and inflicted
she jokes:
"Talk about fucking
a dead horse!"

DUCTS

Quite suddenly the need to cry.
A very strong feeling
and then tears trickling, blurring.
Was there a particular reason
or was it just everything?
It doesn't happen often
no weeping and wailing
just sitting there silently
cheeks covered in salty trails.

To only cry when alone
not because of embarrassment
but grief shared is halved
and that's cheating
both yourself and what
you're grieving for.

That ache in the jaw
fingers smearing wetly
wiping it all away.
Always feel better after
as if you have surmounted
something known or unknown
those hidden darknesses
taking their toll unexpectedly
as if reasons, solid, like ice
are needed for any of us bearing
our souls through our eyes.

REQUEST

Sometime soon
with winter approaching
the feel of it cold upon the skin
spiting the sun but not yet bitter
we will meet and briefly kiss.
Smiles will accompany looks
noticing those slight differences
where we haven't changed a bit.
We will both drink dark ale
eat and drink some more
but most of all we'll talk
as if we are old lovers
joking and teasing, if not regretting.
Maybe there will be a moment
as we both avoid something
almost said but it will pass
and into the fresh blown street
among crisp brown leaves scattering
the air will whiten our words.
We will embrace, kiss and hesitate
wishing to prolong our goodbye
before winter blooms. Let it be
sometime soon.

BUILDING SISYPHUS BUILDINGS

OUT TO LUNCH

The manager starts the reading
bang on time
despite years of experience.

We sit nursing ourselves
into uncomfortable chairs
while cheap wine seeps
into stomachs and carpet tiles.

The shop is busier during this hour
than the rest of its yearly commerce
distracting for the lonely reader
with doors vibratingly clunkered shut
the snaffling of plastic bags
the till's clatter and high-decibel buzz
dot-matrixing every receipt.

Just at that subtle point
where we begin to feign interest
a window cleaner arrives and the manager
helplessly sinks into himself.
Ladders clanking
soap sudding up the glass
the wiping rubber blade's
faintly audible squeaks.
The spectacle alone is too much
neither Lisa St Aubin de Terán
nor her coat can compete.

The manager's world disintegrates
when the Swedes enter
making noise as if it were an art form
translating the visual of sheep into sound.
He's on his feet and creeping swiftly
on soft-soled shoes to hush them

with arm gestures contact is made but
the manager doesn't know the Swedish
for Shhhh!
They seem to think
they are being invited somewhere.
The manager speaks Welsh flawlessly
they speak Swedish LOUDLY!

Smiling defeatedly, the manager knows
satisfaction will be unobtainable
in this transaction
and the only conclusion available
is that modern literature
is just too
quiet.

THE POEM

The the of **the** is **the**
where **the the** is **the**
if there is **the, the** is.
To **the** or not to **the**
that is **the** question.

This **the** that is
is all **the the's**
that ever **the** was
the the that **the** was made for
till **the** do us part.

And if my **the** for **the**
is **the** no longer
I shall play **The The**
till **the** loss is too **the**
and all my **the** is finally **the'd**.

But till then dance **the**
sing **the** and love **the**
for in each **the** we connect
the the to **the** in all our **the**
and if not **the**, then what **the**?

DIS IS JEST TUH SAY LIEK

dat i scoffed
duh sarnee
yoo id in
duh freezuh Kumpartmunt

an wat
yooz wuz praps
kráabin
fuh laytuh like

sorree yuhno
ir wuz jaamtastik
reeuhlee baanaaanaaree
aan reeuhlee baaraaas

(Translated from the American
of William Carlos Williams)

CAT-FLAP

Black cat, cat-flap, flick-flack
lad pad into back yard
shag next door's tabby cat.
After tabby shag lark
whacked, it park napped.
Then snacked, lapped, crapped
and slapped back
flick-flack, cat-flap, black cat.

(to e.e.)

itsa
fourletter
word that
ends in e
and begins
in j
its
middle
is not
(al)right
but
itis
O.K.

ON HAIKU

frog

      ice

              THUD!

BLUE ZOBOLE

For many years
he has spoken without language
has talked up hill and down.
Glowing, luminous, street lights
haunting the blue dark valley
houses, himself, the upside-down dog
those mountains, laughing at gravity
all caught in the moon's X-ray.

Singing this in his ill-fitting jacket
I can feel how flat is my 'big city'
compared to his intermingled land and sky.
"It's good to work in just one colour."
he says, standing awkwardly
surrounded by the blues
of drowned men, of sleepless sea beds
deep in the night's ocean of his earth
tilting the mind to life's negative plate.

20th September, 1994.

AFTER THE FESTIVAL

Suddenly in the headlight's beam
on the road to Brecon
well past Saturday night
a man in shorts and running shoes
                      jogging.

The next night
after the long last day
walking the Nivens to their house
a boy in long trousers lopes past.

Back in The Swan the party's over
Terry Jones is looking even more crumpled
and Kay and Duffy are drunkenly
pendulating up the stairs.

Driving through Hay one last time
people have dissipated to homes and beds.
My engine idles, the streets are alone.

Across the bridge
there are lights at the festival site
but don't disturb them
turn the car finally towards leaving.

After departing
but before being followed
halfway up the Brecons
by the suspicious police
I pass two men in light trousers
and white short-sleeved shirts
                      jogging.

Passing Storey Arms the full moon howls
roller coaster down to a duller world.

FOUR NODDING JOHNS AND AN ASHBERY
for Ifor Thomas on his 50th Birthday

Sitting behind Big John
I become intimate
with the back of his neck.

It is not at all hairy
smooth skin slides up
from shirt collar to hairline.

Angular jowls protrude
in that wide American way
bald patch crowning the silver.

That slim, white, straight scar
flows along the spine but for how far?
Has he had major surgery?

When he starts to read
F.T.Prince has pinched my seat
so from the floor I listen.

His voice, cut from sight
a pure amplified Yankee sound
though he's sat down.

Not minding the heat and no seat
I have a pint of Flowers and the rain
quietly falls outside as his voice does in.

Ifor is stuck horsing in the Park
but I'm enjoying myself;
is it me or is he accessible?

The room is packed
and laughter's gently ruffled
at the appropriate moments.

So what if he's won a Pulitzer
this old soak is, I guess, okay
though he holds his pen a peculiar way.

At the end and embarrassingly
the question and answer section bombs.
In the bar it's Oliver and several Johns.

Cigarettes are bummed, the beeb is thumbed
bankruptcy and the Bay are plumbed
while poets journey through the weather.

But most memorable, his bent back
head halfway down his chest
shoulders a high-rimmed, hard shell.

What slow delivery and deliberate
a Murphy's of language to masticate
Ashbery, sage in his poise, tortoise.

TORRANCE AND THE ART OF BICYCLE MAINTENANCE

Stripping down the broken Raleigh frame
to put the parts on the Pusch replacement
I think of him explaining slowly
that my story was excellent in all areas
except that it didn't have a saddle
and that reading it would hardly be a joy
forcing the rider to do it standing up.

New orange rubber inserted into brake blocks.
Paint applied to cleaned mud guards.
The bicycle spanner as a thing of wonderment
its loss filling me with surprising angst.
The mystery of pedals and of whether
it's better to be one-piece, cottered or cotterless.

The chain lubing in the tin of oil
I remember him praising my essay;
the gleaming frame, the handlebar control
and the comfort of the glossy saddle.
He then remarked the one subtle fault,
that it wouldn't go far without wheels.
A fact stunningly obvious when pointed out
by creative writing's answer to Eddy Merckx.

Poetry was a subject of detailed minutiae.
Yes the bike would work when rusty,
with broken spokes and awkward derailleurs
but its poetry would fail in the long run
leaving you freewheeling into prose
its language cycling well within itself.

The spokes had to be tuned just so.
The right amount of tension in the chain.
The perfect poundage in the pneumatic tyres.
The callipers neither too loose or rubbing.
The saddle adjusted to a height at which
a stationary rider had to lean to touch down.

When all this was calibrated to the individual
then the machine would travel beyond itself
and on some country road both bike and biker
would be transported by their mutual harmony
as a poem moves inexplicably beyond language.

A WHITE STICK
for Gillian Clarke

Thirty thirteen-year-old remedials are creating their own small pandemonium; fighting, throwing things, shouting and banging anything that can be banged which includes heads.

I've done my poems and got an exercise out of them, some of whom didn't even try, just handing in blank sheets of paper. Still, I'd read those out as well; "Blank sheet, blank sheet no.2, blank sheet no.3, I think this could be an epic! blank sheet no.4," etc. They laugh. It's fun, Poetry is fun! So while I'm handing out the cut-out magazine pictures which they have to write a poem about, the teacher leaves the room and the kids erupt. They're all wound up and full of it. If I come on too strong I'll alienate them and because I'm only here for a day I can't afford that. I pull two kids apart and tell them to 'behave'. A girl has written three poems already. A boy who doesn't know what he's supposed to do is asking non-stop, "What am I supposed to do?" and another boy has had his coat thrown out of the window. I tell the girl to do some more, explain to the boy who doesn't know what he's supposed to do, what he is supposed to do and then go and look out of the window. We're only on the ground floor and the coat is lying, rumpled on the grass, close, but quite out of reach. I consider lifting the boy out to get it but instantly feel that it would be the wrong thing to do. I tell the coat-owner to go out the door and around the building to get it. I am very specific in my instructions just in case he has some outlandish route in mind.

As the teacher comes back in they all become noticeably quieter. Soon after that the lad with the coat returns. "Where have you been?" she asks sternly. "Siggsy threw my coat out the window miss and sir told me to go and get it." "Did he now?" and she gives me a brief smile of understanding. I'm just a poet in school to do a reading and workshop. I get to be called 'sir', which always unnerves me, and am looked on by the kids as something special i.e. 'A POET', which unnerves me even more.

They've settled down some and everything seems to be going okay. The ones who handed in blank sheets are all writing except for a long-haired boy at the

146

back. He'd turned up late and missed most of the session. I look over his shoulder to see he's got a picture of several nuns playing snooker.

"What's the problem? Can't think of how to start or what?"

"I can't read or write can I!" he snaps.

"Oh stupid is it?" He looks up at me furiously and I carry on quickly, "I used to be stupid too you know. Yeah! I was in a remedial class as well, teachers used to be always telling me I was thick. Really! Now look at me, a bloody poet eh!" The word 'bloody' sort of impresses him as I knew it would, teachers aren't supposed to say it. I tell him I once got seven in a maths exam and that I'm proud of that because it was the highest mark I ever got for maths. He smiles begrudgingly and makes a half-hearted effort, but he is plainly unable to write and as a writer it always gets to me. Illiteracy is something I am almost fearful of. I have just over an hour to teach him to do poetry in his head, to compose it rather than write it, not that he has a choice. I'd need days, with him on his own, but there's the rest of the class and they also have demands. So I'll do my best and then, probably like everyone else who's tried with him, move on.

When the final bell goes there is the usual madness and then the deserted silence with just me and the teacher left to appreciate it. She tells me the school is going to close down, "Part of the cuts." Knowing this she still makes the effort and does so every day. As for me, I'm glad I only do this once every few months or so. I pack up my books, cards, pictures, etc. and, throat hoarse, walk from the dry heat of the class-room to the chill bite of November. The cold clutching at my breath I stop and look around. School is abandoned.

TEMPORARY DAD

His alarm switched off he snoozes
ignoring daylight and thoughts of school.
"Come on, get up and get dressed."
He snuggles deeper into the duvet.
I pull the cover back. "If you don't get up
I'll throw a bucket of cold water over you!"
"Yeah, right!" He half smiles, burrows deeper.
I go get a saucepan and dribble cold water
just a sprinkle's worth, from the tap.
I carry it in as if it was full, pull the duvet
down and give him one final warning.
"You wouldn't dare." He's so sure that
when I tip the pan and the water sprays around
he jumps. Then realises how little it is.
"Mum'll kill you for this!" I laugh and tell him
"You wet the bed! Now get up or next time
the pan will be full!" He gives me that look
crawls out and reaches for his red top.

Later in the kitchen, eating Rice Krispies,
he smiles at me, milky mouthed, swollen eyed
from sleep and hair all over the place.
He turns back to his Snap, Crackle and Pop
and I think of how adorable he is.
The bowl tipped up, he slurps sweet cereal milk
then puts on his coat, picks up his lunch bag
hugs me and off he goes, almost late for school.
Three weeks till I see him again. A boy at breakfast.
A dad who knows what life is for.

STREWN

When the woman next door screams
I leap the wall and rush in.
As she dials 999, I find my father
lying on the landing, covered in sweat
his rough hands clamped to his chest
his desperate eyes fighting for breath.
Not knowing what to do I hold his head.
"Jesus boy, this is it," he gasps.
Tools and bag are strewn down the stairs
the board he'd tried to lift
ajar beside the attic ladder.
"Hold on," I say, "you'll be alright."
I can see he doesn't believe me.
Suddenly my mother is there
and ambulance men who pick their way
up the stairs to stretcher him down again.
My nephew, hand in mine, grizzles
as my mother goes with my father.

Phone calls full of fear to the family.

My sister, in slippers, running down the street.

At the hospital we immediately get lost
till in a dim-lit space I spot my brother.
We do the worst thing we can do
we wait and joke that it's okay.
Everywhere is polished emptiness.
"Just five days past his three score and ten
not much is it?" My brother out-stares neon.
I see a nurse I know but don't wish to talk to.

My mother, who's been in there with him
comes out, the doctor's arm on her shoulder.
This is worse than her shocked white face.

He turns away, she walks up to us
says too loud, "Silly ruddy sod!"
She's obviously in shock.
"He's only wrenched some bloody
chest muscles!" She is livid.

As my father is probed by doctors
my sister is on the floor in the corridor
wheezing asthmatically and failing
to use her inhaler because of laughter.
My brothers and I cannot control ourselves
and my mother, by now, is also laughing
though she still looks as if
she could kill him for this.

WING MIRROR

The day's clarity is that of March
sun bright and lucid.
Bill Way's scrapyard resonates with a tang
my Polish hobnails, impervious to sharp metal
squelching black oil mud
around double and triple-stacked cars
looted of parts in a wilful decay.
I hope to prize a window panel out
to get back at my Maxi's vandals.

Unwashable grime-pitted index finger.
Cremated home-made lasagne darkly crisped.
Molars grinding black crunchy pasta
with softening soft brown bread
gulped cuttingly down weary gullet.
Glass plate molten rimmed with cheese weld.
Stomach howling like a scrapyard dog.

In the backstreet lane I push glass out
shattered cubes scatter across tarmac.
Twisting and pulling new window into rubber
into place only, swearingly, to discover
the wing mirror, pocketed and unpaid for
is, like myself, the wrong size and shape.

LEFT-HAND DRIVE

She gave me this ball-point pen
that screws instead of clicks.
It made up for the god-awful Japanese cookies
and the book she bought me
but never showed me
because I already had it.
I will forever wonder what it was.

After arriving at Cardiff station
sat, pensively in my red maxi
so lightly we kissed
so badly we wanted
that flicker of time so breathless.
"I think I've forgotten how to make love."

Newly washed hair frissioned with grey.
That white outfit, light and shade glasses.
Topless, chest down, floral skirt crumpled over cheeks
back, lean, head side-on against Swan's pillow
thighs that I love and she doesn't show
because she hates them.

The cliff-top at the bottom of her street
past midnight, past the garden for the blind
surrounded by the moving sea darkness.
I couldn't tell her I loved her
not in Scarborough.

At the end of Stratford, eating Greek
"I'm going to miss you, you know."
she said as if it were some big confession.
I knew everything would go wrong
if she didn't phone.

The first time she declared
'I love you', it was in London
written on a postcard
found in my hotel bathroom
after she had left.
She even had the decency
to give me glandular fever.
What was that she shouted?
"We love you Charlie English!"

BRITTLE PETAL

In Hay you gave it quickly
snapped the stem in a twist
in a rare spontaneous gesture.

Carefully car put and kept
we parted for separate journeys
but the flower nestled my dashboard.

In Cardiff I hung it upside down
as I'd seen another woman do
thought of Scarborough and you.

Thorough though our affair was
throughout that too brief summer
as love bloomed, the flower dried.

A year since I last saw you
another since we first met
I notice it hanging, forgotten till…

Slip knot from stem, take it down.
Damp, white and green is dry, light brown.
Amidst brittle petals, purple blood freckles.

Unyielding flower would snap not bend
and nothing gives but the memories.
Into so many mistakes, how did we break?

No smell now, would crush if held tight
yet I long to smell it, feel soft petals light
as I long to smell you, feel soft petals wet.

WRITING TO MYSELF

Your parcel was returned today
unopened, all its contents safe,
two years since I sent it.

Circling it as it had circled back
I read the many scrawlings
across my neat address.

I open it and the letter
postcards, photo's, books and posters
fall out like wounded birds.

The inscriptions with love, the poems
that I know now you've never seen
and suddenly all that silence makes sense.

It wasn't you that gave up but me.
That I, in sad anger, didn't keep up
with more letters, just the unanswered phone.

How useless all this is, these gifts ungiven,
my sentiments expressed only to myself,
your heart hardening because I didn't.

So if I send you this, now, will it
be too late, your house moved out of,
this sorry missive returned unopened?

LLANISHEN

With the foundations dug, the cement lorries arrive.
Seven in all, neatly spaced during the long day
to vomit their churned cement into the trenches
to pile it high in one spot as wheels sink in soft earth.

At the first, wielding shovels like samurai, we leap in
frantically channelling the slop to awkward corners
before, sun drenched, it dries or another load arrives.
Kids are running, jumping, falling, bespattered, wailing.

When a dark cloud blooms, damp earth wafts
rain spots tingle through shirts hot with work
Ifor, Andy, Karl and me, up to our knees in it
the cold grey sludge flowing to hold a house steady.

By afternoon the cement has seeped to my ankles
drying, it will harden and grittily rub the skin
sandpapering through indifference to aches and pains.
Stripped to the waist, backs burn, muscles contract.

After the sixth lorry's rotating snail shell is emptied
our energy seriously depleted, ploughing on but sinking
dripping towards the final load, we pace our weariness.
Gnats bite, blood hums, we can taste the day's closing.

With blisterless hands I undress for the running bath
my aching back is itchy but not burnt too badly
removed socks reveal two red rings, worn and bloody.
Would it feel something like this to have worked in chains?

THE REMOVAL MAN'S RECURRING BALLET COMPANY

Electric typewriters, personal knick-knacks
lamps unplugging, desks unscrewing
baker's pallets full of confidential files
swivel top, rockable chairs on rollers.

Cold, green, metal filing cabinets
drawers first, numbered and lettered
the manhandling up circular stairs.
Is going up a form of travel?

Even after its legs have been removed
all four of us around and around
the dark wood of the conference table
executive decisions weighing heavily.

The hands become dry and hot
blistering on metal edges
receiving unvarnished wood's splinters.
Removal men feel the bottom of everything!

Confusion and several people in charge
lead to a full, eight-foot filing cabinet
being lifted, dragged and sworn at
only to go back to its original place.

The free lunch is beef, egg, cheese, ham
salmon and shrimp with mayo sandwiches
but Ben doesn't want any, he's religious
officially he works for Pickfords.

Tightness across the chest
a welter of sweat and dust
the pining ache of leg muscles
my back clicking as I straighten.

Working in two's, toing and froing
constant tea to get our liquids back
there's talk of how the "Big Bopper
ad more go in im than Elvis ever ad."

"Look at these map cabinets Ken
from the Marquis of Bute, made in the castle.
God knows why we ever bought them
but they have seen good service."

The five-foot square partition's top
hits a low, unseen beam unexpectedly
jolts forcibly into my collar bone
jars me painfully to my knees.

We've moved their office furniture
one floor up, now they move personal things
little items and comforts till where they are
seems the same as where they came from.

A new geography is slipped on
like another dress or suit
preserving their inner stability
settling in to an unchanging perspective.

The cold outside cleans and soothes
like putting down a heavy object
that's been held far too long.
Cash in hand is received with smiles.

Knowing we've done for the day
we practise easing up in the Jubilee
where I fondle my dark pint
and my sore swollen shoulder.

SETTING THE RECORDS ON FIRE

In the cool, dust-laden tomb of the basement
tying twine, pulling it just so every time
two small blisters appear on each little finger
where shows the strain of tightened knots.

The files bundled, we stack them upstairs
and then hump them across hard hot pavement
to a hired van parked on double yellow lines.
We load it till the wheels rub the arches.

But this is not waste-paper; legally, it has to burn
so the next morning we're at British Petroleum
using their huge outdoor incinerator in July heat.
Sweltering, ashes swirling, smoke choking, we drip.

A van full and we left loads behind to be kept
and this is the second time it's been done this year.
Hauling folders 10 to 15 years old but still worth
firing into a blaze so fierce you can't breathe near it.

We're burning the evidence, but evidence to what?
Property foreclosures, dodgy land deals, developments
contracts sealed, deeds done, lives undone and done up.
Or are they a testament to the honesty of estate agents?

Days from now the records will still be alight
their white smoke environmentally safe so they say
and of what has burnt out among the smouldering ashes
there is no justice, only an equal destruction.

BUILDING SISYPHUS BUILDINGS

Ploughing the wheelbarrow
full of slurping cement
through brick-dirt mud
grime polished, rust-pocked handles
not as sure as solid
straining gripping hands
balancing unseen tyre
up bend wobbling planks
the 'hup' and jerk, up-ending
resting weight on barrow bumper bar
holding it from over tipping too far
that moment with nothing
but the waiting.
Finally the cement sloughs out
polloping into itself like porridge.
Handles are relaxed back
barrow trundles down plank
crosses rough ground bouncing
to where shovelfuls await its filling
and the routine is replayed endlessly
both barrow and man are worked
till age or breakage renders them redundant
to be replaced with another man or barrow
to wheel cement now and ever after.

SUBDUED

We stand in the queue subdued
by the bland niceness bequeathed
by John Major's 'Citizen's Charter'
the sycophantic semantics of 'reception area'
the carpets, the soft décor, the pallid lighting
the odiousness of false friendship.

I remember the grills and plastic windows
the sick-coloured paint jobs
the stainless matt floor tiling
and the nauseous-orange chairs
that unmistakable hospitalised effect
as if to suggest we weren't well
certainly not well enough or else
we wouldn't be there, gravitating
towards the Giro's bleak anaesthetic.

At least then there was a sense of oppression
something to not get ground down about
fighting back the shit-hole mentality with anger
but now we've had even that removed
by padded seats and Yucca rubber plants.

Now we know the names behind the faces
behind the open-plan computerized counters
and as our seventeen page, four colour
cost a small fortune to print, signing-on booklet
is produced only to be glanced at
so that we may sign and be bar coded
I know that we, the great sub-civilisation
have become less than overlooked
we've been seen
acknowledged slightly for selfish ends
and then ignored
like a Jobcentre notice-board.

UNDER THE BRIDGE

1. BIRD'S SCRAPYARD

Under industrial sky
my off-white Marina estate
half its propshaft missing
thirty quid.
Bird's in the rain
every car I've ever owned
is represented here
banged up
      broken down
some almost whole
others desiccated
Cortina Mark 1
Triumph Herald Convertible
Hillman Hunter
Sunbeam Talbot
even the ones I sold
probably scrapped now.
Oil smearing
acetylene flaring
damp metal tang
burnt rubber
      sodden wool.
Hair plastered
      breath fogging
water atmospheres
      arrayed on eyelashes
the monotonous
      drip and drop.

2. THE SPILLER BUILDING

In Rover Way
no car now
just plodding footslap
      westwards
from Bird's and Blackshore.
Wind bite sight seared
Spiller's tall white building
standing alone
like a beacon amongst
the demolished.
Roath docks sullen liquid
shortcut through emptiness
eyesore fly-tipped garbage
alongside stone and brick
      rubbled.

Balancing dry
      dock gate
hands grip cold rail
I look down
murkiness
my reflected head
      wavers there.
Sod him
      his stupid stare
spit in his smeary eyes
ripples obliterate him
carefully I shuffle across.

On the dock bankside
stride solidly
the long oblique
      walk back
to a cold home.

3. PIERHEAD

Around the old docks
under cranes
beside rusting ships
in huge rectangles
of torpid water
misery depressing
intruding the jobless
        internal void.

No part of my city
do I own
even my soul
is rented.
Rain spits
        hunched forward
Roath basin dock
my grampy Jack
in charge of all metal
during the war
the last time
        it thrived
now it's just a chasm
        to drown all hope.

Redbrick Pierhead
a museum of nothing
glared at severely
by arterial mud
channelling
        bay tides
slum pumping
till the barrage
plugs Cardiff's
        life support.

4. SCHOONER WAY

Hemingway Road
succubus to Atlantic Wharf
the oriental effect
      Council offices
sucking drivel dry.

Along Schooner Way
the houses new
      vacant
paint already peeling
Winter wind stripping
      sham glossiness.

The few trees
have wood bark
instead of soil
even the designer earth
      faked.

This bleak middle-class
media plump
      city estate
just one dark tunnel
from old Tiger Bay
filleted by planners
      kebabbed.

Ducks paddle
      Bute East dock
already unfit
      for human swimmers.

5. ATLANTIC WHARF

Eben Haezer
MAAIKE Maru
Old Rotterdam
     sailing barges
slicked up
     decorative
moored alongside
     'The Wharf'
pretend rail pub
mockneyed station
Sarum hardwood
     cracking
not painted properly
lichened green algae.

Follow the playtime
dock feeder canal
too small
     for boats
a few feet wide
planner's romantic
dream waterway
     concrete
     cement
no aquatic curves.

Inertly wander
traipsing through
newness
houses block designed
without shops
     for ghosts
uninhabitable
     without
automobiles.

6. TYNDALL STREET

The Celtic Bay Hotel
another warehouse
      tarted up
I go in for a pint
directed to the
      cocktail bar
      don't bother
leave gaudiness
for outer cold
at least the wind
      isn't pretending
to be something else.

I stand outside
      looking
I worked on it
      years ago
with dad and Rob
lead gullies ripped out
stolen for scrap
so we boarded it up
waterproofed it
high up gazing
at emptiness
      wasteland
from here to the shipless
Bute East dock
like the aftermath
      of world's end.

Now it's full
human storage
so expensive
I couldn't afford
      to live here
just gaze in awe
      drift past.

7. THE BRIDGE

Under warehouse sky
metal roll up doors
secured weathered
unkempt signed
Aston and Fincher
BSS
AA Frozen Food
TODAY'S, The New Warwick
Kayes (Cardiff) Ltd.
ROCK BOTTOM WHOLESALE.

Follow feeder canal
cross Tyndall Street
      meet it again
through fly-tipped
      brambles
used rubbers
      broken pram
smell stone mould
      stale urine
into darkness
      under bridge
railings blocked end
      railway lines.

Feeder water underground
      under rails
here I stand at the arse
of another Winter
      on the dole
under the bridge
      uniquely arched
hyper paraboloid
      split brick
barrel vaulting

magnificent
hidden by darkness
what a wondrous
              dead end.

AUTUMN DAY

Lord it is time. The summer was so grand.
Lay long shadows on the sundials
and let the wind free upon the land.

Command slow fruit to ripen on the vine;
grant them two clear days more,
to fill their cups up brim full and pour
the final sweetness into the heavy wine.

Whoever is homeless now, will never have a home.
Whoever is alone now, will remain alone,
will wake, read, write till late a poem
and will in alleyways, up and down,
restlessly wander, where brown leaves are blown.

(Translated from the German of
Rainer Maria Rilke)

LARYNX

The first time I met Llewellyn
he offered me Afghanistan money,
a note travelled and tattered,
limply held together by a sticking plaster,
in exchange for my slight book of poems.
Later he showed me his photographs;
khaki clad, stiff, posturing with guns,
Action Man in a mercenary costume
but with spectacles.

The Afghani villagers treated him like a prince
gave him their best rice, festooned with beetles
but all they had. He ate it gladly, honoured.
He knew what he was fighting for there
so, full of it and drunk, he wouldn't let me go,
kept talking, taking incoherence into uncomfortableness,
to the point where everyone left him to it.

***   ***   ***

Months later, Llewellyn turns up reciting poetry,
wallowing in lost nationalism, Welsh mythology
and warriors in the mist to justify
his recent excursion to Sarajevo.

In the badly typed manuscript
thrust at me that night
his early idealism soon capitulated
and reasons fell apart.
With no easily identifiable transgressor,
confusion and then survival took over.
He did as he was told until injured
and invalided out, though he's pulled
the wrong trigger and knows it.

***   ***   ***

The last time I saw him
he was singing a song in Welsh
which he'd written himself
though, like all he does now, failing
where he most wants to clear a path.

Drunk and excitable, in the bar,
he demonstrates how to kill,
but can't say why the elbow-forearm
should smash into the larynx.
He shows me not once but repeatedly,
in fast replay, his mind locked,
unable to get it out in mere words.
He's desperate to connect Wales to Bosnia
with the scar hotly skating
down his deviated forehead,
which we are unable to get into.
He's unable to say it in either tongue
but what if he could?

SWIMMING IN THE LIVING ROOM

It is while watching the mystics
failing to display their levity on TV
that from the floor in the room's corner
I slowly kick-off and glide shark-like
across the rug's oriental pattern.
Then, just before the crumpled sofa
I arch my back and curl upwards
rising past bookshelves to float
upside-down and inches below the ceiling.

Bosnia's imploding, Britain's running on empty
looking elsewhere as the American dream
hamburgers the world into submission.
We are all slaves to the left hand
of god's television; panic, after all, is natural.
The great working-class T-shirt proclaims
'DIE YUPPIE SCUM' as the ineffable
South American Realists
ponder the Welsh question again?
Kitchens are only gravitational
as the heavy tap
on the back of the head proves
while every politician's body has enough sulphur
to rid one dog of fleas
Cwmdonkin Park is just a wasteland
and every book must have its misprints.
'62% of the population believe they are working-class'.
The children of Grangetown are singing
the death knell of Billy the Seal.
The tortoise of Judas Iscariot is voting Tory
the fat man is relishing pubic hairs with mustard
and poetry is just a window-squashed face.

As our barraged homes become sea-bed wrecks
sprawling above my desk
lilting with the water's motion
the slip of a job centre form
turning to mulch drifts by.

CLODHOPPERS

1.

Hunched over
pulling the heels
then the stiff little stamp
as the socked foot
slips in.
Feel the sole cold
stamp the whole foot
boot and all.
Satisfied with the grip
I pull the loops of the laces
tightening the leather
to that neat bow
just above the ankle line
far too dainty
for the monstrosity below.
As soon as that's done the bell goes
and outside a van waits.
Standing I'm aware
of my new solidity
I walk rigidly to the door
careful not to leave
mouldings of yesterday's work
on the linoleum.
My balance slightly askew
feet firmly the day begins.

2.

Hunched over
pulling the heels
loosening the leather
then the strain
muscles tautening stomach
it slips off suddenly
to reveal the warm damp
of a sock stuck to a foot.
Wiggle the toes deliciously
pull the cloying material
rub the ball and instep
set the foot on cold lino
let its cool melt into the sole.
Both boots weighty in hand
the soft inner leather furry
the hard outer pebbled
blocked tread for grip
45, made in Poland.
Carry them smudged and caked
with dried and drying mud
to their corner, ready
for the morrow's labour
and head for the bath
leaving two sweaty imprints
evaporating like a physical act.

ROOFING

1. FIRST DAY

Early morning
back on top
snowflakes falling slowly
darkness waning quickly
doing this job for my sister
my father getting out the old tools
remembering what was thought forgotten.

Cold hands blue as the sky
feet numb on ladder rungs
mind crisp with fear.

Not enough planks
to cover the scaffolding
a walkway with 'traps'
I put my hand over the low sun
snow dribbles
ice slurries.

Smashing and 'ripping'
slates and battens
hurling them into the chasm
between houses
dust whirls to sting eyes
clog noses and choke throats.

Simon and Stephan
are on the fiddle
Stephan listens, thinks, learns
but Simon has a wife and kid
wants to get it over with
a true hobbledihoy
he breaks two rungs on the ladders
my father's had for twenty years.

Naked joists point at a clear cold sun
which shows their frailness
their rottenness which we have to fix
but we can't, so we just 'make good'
bolster them up as best we can
then cover them with plastic sheeting
criss-crossed with wire
and government specified
it's cheaper than felt
rots the wood quicker
and is more dangerous
being easier to slip on when wet.

At the end of the first day
we've covered and battened
most of three sides
coming down, my night vision fails
in the moonless November black
I rest my body's weight on a nail
which pops through my rubber glove
to pierce the left palm's tendon.

2. TERRY

Waiting for my tetanus
the stark emptiness of casualty
is filled by Terry the drunk
entering like an actor
missing his cue.

In a similar fashion he once
burst in on a poetry reading
I was attempting to do
yellow World Cup Spain '82 jumper
pushing his wife in her wheelchair
both of them hysterically drunk
he shouted, laughed, joked
captivated my audience
took no notice of me
or my devastatingly ineffective
comebacks for hecklers
they just carried on
oblivious until escorted out.

I sit, nursing my swollen hand
hoping he won't remember me.
He marches to reception
demands to see Pat, his wife
who, so the nurse politely informs
has already gone home taxi wise.
He swears loudly
bangs his fist on the counter
violently kicks a chair
that is bolted to the floor
swears even louder
and limps out.

3. PATTERN

Hand throbbing
wrapped in a plastic bag
I continue nailing battens
measurements must be precise
they have to match the slates
mistakes are near impossible
to rectify later.

Although the days pass slowly
the mornings become easier
my body fitting the work pattern
left hand healing quickly.

In his sixties my father
climbswings up the scaffolding
no ladders, safety line or net
hands and feet astretch to cold bars
even a monkey would be envious.

More scaffolding erected, ladders too
we sway, our movements, three storeys up
cause sudden grabs to steady ourselves
getting used to height is dangerous
if you're afraid, you're careful.

The gables
fascia boards, soffit boards, etc.
may be quaint from the ground
but up here they're junk.
Built in 1889
the Welsh slates go
and the gables stay
chucking out the good
keeping the bad.

At the end of the first week
the last of the old slates and dust
are gone and I know that eventually
I will pick out all the black snot.

4. PUZZLE

The flatness of asbestos slates
smooth their puzzle
across the roof
rain, which cannot solve it
sits in globules.
This only happens on a new roof.

5. STOLEN

My father on the ground
me on the edge of the roof
leaning over
not quite far enough
he swings underarm
and the tape measure
hurtles upwards
three storeys
to rest in space.
Before it can begin
its decent
it sits on nothing
until I reach out my hand
and gently steal it
from gravity.

6. FLAT LIGHT

Sitting on the crest
I realize just how flat
Cardiff is
a calm sea of chimneys
broken by a few
lonely skyscrapers
all the way to
Caerphilly
Rumney
Leckwith
and Penarth.

Below
coupied down
cutting lead
for the roof's valleys
my father's extended
steel tape measure
snickers and crackles
as it reels itself in
snaking into his hand
a lightning strip
flashing.

7. OVERFLOWING

Hands scarred and rough
grime worn into their prints
they go red then blue
rain warms the atmosphere
but ensures they are kept
damp and thus cold
numbness only ceases when
the hammer prefers their nails.

Pissing down
water flurries across the roof
overflowing soft-soled shoes
soaking bums
drenching every uncovered part
work becomes farcical
as the overhangs and gutters
shoot rain down necks.

Leaving it unfinished
we go home depressed
knowing there's a lot more to do
and that it will rain tomorrow
and for the next few days.

8. EACH OTHER

Simon and Stephan have gone
my father and I carefully slate
the awkwardness of gables.

The great diagonal crosses the roof
until we crowd each other
into one last unslated corner.

AFTER STOLICHNAYA CHASERS

WORLD CUP

Micheal McGann's wife has left him,
taken the raucous kids from blocking his vision
and fled from his fundamentalist fandom.

The final row, through screams and tears, when
to her incomprehension his job was jacked in,
in order to devote himself to match mania.

He's filled the vacuum of their leaving
with seven rented television sets
tuned in, in every room; even the smallest.

He won't miss a tap, a flick or a foul,
nor a penalty save or offside goal,
nor the rain spray from the back of the net.

Every slo-mo will be euphoric.
Every bead of sweat from a missed header.
Every cursed-at referee gesture.

Such is his obsessive vigilance
he's just a tube sucked inside out
teetering into mid-life soccer insanity.

With his children and his wife gone,
his low-paid job, his life gone,
his house is a blur of television glare.

And when the World Cup is over, what then?
Nothing to watch but his empty life?
"Oh no," glints he, "I've got it all on DVD!"

MUSIC FOR WINE LOVERS

Angle me the bottle of blue and red
see love's lips, juicy pasta
permanganate, autumn.
Dancing off of the off-beat
making love to the rising glug bubbles
green spilling red onto blue tongue
happiness in miasma and swirl.

Called her up and she was sober.
Bigger fool her and told her so
so now we're officially finished.
Isn't that what drunkenness is for?
Not caring when they breathalyse you.
Not worrying about contraction.
Not breaking anything down three flights
and all because the taste of shiraz undulates.

Whirling the skipping rope, pissed and hopping.
All that forgotten dreck that comes at you
from the depths of wine stains and regret.
Hold yourself under and gulp till you stop
red being so much prettier than luck.

AMBITION

Having not really decided
that going downhill
is better than going up
he's on the slide
forever sleeping though breakfast
then gently coasting awake
to spend the afternoon
in pyjamas and unshaved.
He cooks sausages in the oven
because he can't be bothered to fry
and if by six a few bottles of wineasy
have also gone downhill
then at least his standards
are being rigorously maintained.
By evening, however, he is failing
always too drunk or
not quite drunk enough
nodding off in a dreamless armchair
his head is on one side
his life is full of unfinished bookshelves
his god has gone out square dancing
and how he wishes his slippers
could be cremated.
He can hear through the thin walls
the indistinct voices of people next door
failing to talk about him.
Beauty is such a sham
but till then why worry when
the corkscrew is looking to be found.

LAURA'S SATURDAY NIGHT

Poppadoms
cracking edges
cutting into fingers
faint linger of fat
nostrilating
wet card-like
tongued.

Awaiting madras
they enter;
lacquered hair
white shoes
fake leather handbags
and distorted faces
rainbows of warpaint.

"Oy! Wee waans sum kurrees rite
aan wee wans tuh bee sirvd faast like
aan weel aav for kaampaari an liems
aan wee aayunt goanna wayt fur em see
aan ewe messus ubowt wog feetyers
aan ners goanna bee uh fukkin rukkus
RIET!"

They are politely seated.
Our steaming food arrives.

As we eat
the inevitable floorshow
at their table
                        unfolds.

THE PARTHIANS INVADE HAY

The publisher is drunk and running.
He circumnavigates the cars.
It is well past midnight
that indecipherable late hour
as we stand in the tilted car park
watching the publisher running.
He runs straight into a hedge
a thing unimaginable to him.
Flailing, sinking, surrounded
by foliage he wonders
what it is? Why it is?

The drunken publisher gets free,
leans on a car and slips off.
He gets up, leans and
slips off again, shouts
at us to stop moving the car.
The car is not moving.

A drunken poet comes up
steadies the publisher, shouts
"NO" repeatedly until
the message penetrates.
Poets make better drunks
than publishers.

Earlier in hospitality,
a fenced-off VIP area
was practically demolished
as the six bottles of free
champagne he'd emptied
were lobbed about
like glass grenades.
Tables were overturned
in an attempt to stand

and then he staggered out
assuaged in a wake
of catering destruction.

Further up the car park
another poet slumps
into his car and farewells.
The publisher is running out
his silent movie needs motion
dissolving into the black lane
he discovers sound and his voice
howls from the darkness
urges us on to the camp-site where
he has arranged tents for everyone.

KINGFISHER BLUE

It was sex like Hitchcock
gone bad in the seventies
in colour, in the shower,
the curtain rings in tatters,
the soap completely unobtainable,
the feet sliding the puckered rubber
as the sweat wet bodies
clasp to the cold malt tiles.
Her long blonde hair slaps his face,
his short black hair ruffles her armpit.
Her sharp teeth serrates his knuckles,
his straight white teeth grates her nipples.
The alcohol brings them down with cries,
the yanked nozzle clatters.
Their final palpitations shudder
through the early hours like slow death
till their heart beats quieten and they listen
as the hotel manager politely knocks.

THE NIGHT BIG FRANK WON THE TITLE
for Diane

"I can't believe I'm listening to this."
said his new girlfriend as he strained
to hear the radio over the pub's din.
The result washed down in disbelief
with poor, fake, Irish beer, because
he'd been too late for the 'Old Speckled Hen'
because they had been 'shaggin'.

After, because she, and now he, is 'veggie',
there was no curry or chips or pastie,
but hummus, coleslaw and Ryvita.
This on top of the sweaty badinage
of over-indulgent, drunken, heat-wave sex,
had him crapping well past midnight,
a thing he never does, and with
embarrassing noisiness at that!
All loud farts punctuated by
small, plummeting balls of excreta
with none of the usual, big solid stuff.

A long, lonely, sleepless hour later,
in the kitchen for a desperate coffee,
a fart splutters into a bobble of squishy turd.
There is not even a cardboard tube
in the kitchen towel dispenser's empty arms
and the living room is totally devoid
of Kleenex, newspaper or brown curtains.

Moving only from the knees down,
with buttocks firmly clenched,
he faces the steep, creaking staircase.
'If Bruno can do it,' he thinks, 'so can I.'
Cheeks clamped, amazingly they hold
till he reaches the toilet's sanctuary
and the mother of all Andrex rolls.

In bed, listening to a distant cock crowing,
the echo of horse's hooves along the street
and the faint bat-flutter at her window,
he is anxious at every tiny, tense release of gas,
of which there are many, and worries
about the possibility of leaving, as he once did,
years before and was never forgiven for,
a male brown skidmark on the female white sheets.

RUTH ON THE ROOF

RUTH!

RUTH!

RUTH!

What are you doing on the roof
RUTH?
Come down off the roof
RUTH!
Is that a bottle of Vermouth
RUTH?
You shouldn't be drinking Vermouth
on the roof
RUTH!
You might fall and break a tooth
RUTH!
Come down off the roof
RUTH!
Just because you're lost your youth
RUTH!
What do you mean I'm being uncouth
RUTH!
I'm not being uncouth
RUTH
Forsooth
RUTH!
It's the truth
RUTH!
No I can't give you proof
RUTH!
Come down off the roof
RUTH!
Stop being a goof
RUTH!

RUTH!

RUTH!

RUTH?
Where are you
have you taken to the hoof
RUTH?
This is just a bit too aloof
RUTH!
You've gone from the roof
RUTH!
What have you done with the Vermouth
RUTH?
Is this some kind of spoof
RUTH?

RUTH!

RUTH! !

RUTH! ! !

OHHHHH
STREWTH !

THE LAST DRUNK IN THE PUB

aav yews eva bin in luuv
wid sumwon oo luuvs anuduh
nowin deyul nevuh bee yowers
pienin koz dey uh wid anuduh

aav yews eva felt daat payun
duh sikunin won dat nors
tyernin yuh insieds
klorin at duh baak uh yuh frowt

aave yews eva kurst yuhself
hert flowin liek aassid rayun
felt trew lownleenus swolo yew up
mayd uh room emptee biee yuh presuns

aav yews eva kurst def
koz ir kud wiep owt eevun luuv
aytid orl forts koz dey no
der won way owts too eezee

aav yews eva endluslee eksplaynd tuh yuhself
wiee yews doan reeuhlee luuv dem
aow yewul ger ova dem in tiyum
dow eevun deyur sheeaado berns

aav yews eva bitun yuh tung
aan wundud wiee der ownlee fing yew feeyuls
iz zaat dey aar nort wif yoo
luuv nulifiyin orl udur payun

aav yews eva sufud wen dey didunt corl
kerst an swor an aytid dem an yuhself
ownlee tuh bee instuntlee apee at der voys
til dey tels yew dey doan luuv yew

aav yews eva.......................

AFTER STOLICHNAYA CHASERS

Into the dawn's bright narcosis
I stagger drooling
ungainly, flat-footed, stiff-legged
joints apoplexing
the piercing grin of light
shifting the sand in my bowels
lulling the bladder's distend.
Eyes are scoured with ick and goo
mouth a stainless-steel tablespoon
rimmed with the gum of envelopes.
To bend is to feel warping pain
as it sickles from neck to temples
a helmet of internal strobe-light.
The achievement of non-movement
is a stasis to be prayed for.
Anaemically hunched over Earl Grey tea
I sit tentatively sipping the liquid button
and wait in eternal limbo
for the bodily Armageddon
of life's knee-jerk vomit to begin.

UNDERWATER

THIRTEEN WAYS OF LOOKING AT TONY CONRAN

I

Among snowy Welsh mountains
only one moving thing
the eye of Conran.

II

He is of three minds
like a poem in which there's
language, subject and other.

III

The world turns
Conran meditates
born in India of ex-patria
now our lingual guru.

IV

Greedy sleek, spy eyed
scavenger blackbird
squawking, collecting
glittering mouthfuls
of bright shining words
in poems to hide.

V

Ley lined monolith
scarred and gnarled
on a harsh, sleet hillside
soft sun and hard rain
keening the bardic winds.

VI

Hair in sparse white strands
like falling rain translated
by ice into crystal snowflakes.

VII

Conversation gained
as your slow brain tuned
into his staggered speech
understanding eased
a joy for both.

VIII

Crow, hood, Conran
claw, beak and song
which isn't which
till the song grips.

IX

Long-distance translations
whale deep songs
vibrating oceans
traversing generations
finding anew
what was thought lost.

X

Intense wingspan
circumnavigator
eerie albatross
we see a fraction
of his capabilities.

XI

Far under the valley
he mines riches
bringing poems to light
the soul of Wales.

XII

Hops to ale
apples to cider
grapes to wine
grain to whiskey
words to lullaby
Conran conjures.

XIII

His beloved ancient ferns
sway from viridescent green
to flowing dark crimson
nature, like genius
can translate anything.

THE PACK
i.m. Iwan Llwyd

A gabble of drunk poets
boistering the country lane
moon crisp and ground hard
the air alive with laughter
literary allusion and bad jokes.

Feeling the moment's ripeness
Muldoon, of all people, says
"Let's run!" and as one we do
breaking into a jogging trot
this unlikely band of warriors
clumping down the unlit tarmac
the short distance to the hostelry
a horde of word hoarders
releasing the tribal magic.
To the closing some take off
a cacophony of sprints and shouts
Muldoon wheezing, stitching come apart
flapping along in his brown wool suit
the two Ifors trying to race Armitage
Twm just about keeping up
Finch frantically waving his torch
Minhinnick way back, glassy eyed
bent against a five-bar gate
Iwan straggling, hat held loosely in hand
singing plaintively into the hedgerows.

Through the gate's finishing line
we stagger about gasping
spewing white clouds and swear words.
Peter Read holds up his shoes
their soles flapping uncontrollably
we start howling like lost wolves
chorusing the empty moon.

Dogs from surrounding farms
join in and the howling ripples out
from dog to dog across North Wales
and farmer's wives nudge husbands
to stumble, be-slippered in muddy darkness
with loaded shotguns and heads full
of the most poetic Welsh blasphemy.

THE IMMORTAL DONKEY JACKET

i.m. Nigel Jenkins

At first he wore the badge
of denim jacket and jeans
long centre-parted hair
typical bearded hippy
as if Punk had never happened.

He'd done it traditional style
trekked to Morocco
worked across the USA
in a circus of all things.

This amiable bard of Mumbles
made every trip to Swansea full
of poetry, gossip and drinking.
Its most popular poet
since Dylan Thomas
a tabloid comparison
he wouldn't thank me for.

The denim was one day
surprisingly upgraded
to a donkey jacket with
patterned shoulders
a splash of colour
on the workman ordinary
that he became known for
and seemed to be eternal.

So after the usual
long-winded phone call
I drove to Mumbles
and failed like so many to find
the house with no front door
just a back lane and his laughter.

Driving to Patrick's luxurious
rustic deco farm, we talked
Union business and directions.
Our late arrival made the meeting
both quorate and inebriate
but added ribaldry and wit.

Several hours and sliced mutton
later I steered us down mountains
to the winding Swansea valley
in summer's low afternoon sun
listening to Nigel's verbal travelogue
voice like the rumbling ocean floor
revealing the archaeology, geology
history, legends, battles, murders
rustling and wrangling, who and how
lived where, which poet or rock star
the endless detail of what he knew
I took in with dumbfounded rapture.

After dropping him off I headed
to Cardiff along motorway blandness
allowing time to reflect how impressed
I was by how intimate he was
with his places and people
that he could sing it all so lovingly
a depth of communal understanding
to aspire to and an inspiration
of what a true poet could be.

THE THIRD DATE

ONE

From Mulligan's to the free open-air concert
there was an uneasy, kinetic anticipation.

They pretended to like the music, arms encircled
followed by strolling the funfair, hands held.

At his suggestion she accepted a lift home.
He had made all the right moves, she had let him.

He was already sat in the car, key fiddling
when she showed him the smashed window glass.

An hour searching with a too weak torch
recovered her bag, some contents, his shirt, but

her money and his new suit had legged it leaving
just the glass to despondently cut themselves on.

Sat on newspapers, her shoulder to the wind
he drove a torpid fifty, a motorway gale inside.

It could have been a bad end to a good night
but wasn't until they fell asleep before they started.

TWO

Throat a raging virus from their bacteria swap
a mile walk across the sand dunes a minor Sahara.

The bag contained a mess of food neither wanted
and a bottle of warm wine they'd foolishly drunk.

The excremental globbed, brown foamed sea
was duly paddled in and then washed off in a pool.

After a longer trek back, stopping for dune berries
the pint of Wadsworth's Glory in The Prince was acrid.

At her place they squashed into the bath together
salt, sand and stickiness soothingly combined with cramp.

Initially refreshed, towelling down they rubbed
each other up the right way till arousal's carrot

found them having sex that was far too prolonged
they were slipping overboard in sweat-sore weariness.

Tired and unable to want to say what was wrong
they sat up, drank coffee, created future's crumbs.

THREE

After running, in mid-day heat, around Mumbles hills
unfalteringly lost and increasingly desperate with lateness

the long drive and the much longer Union meeting
with too much of the extremely weak lager he'd brought

he called, as he'd said, to see her on his way home.
Thankfully her teenage daughter confirmed she was out.

He drove to The Prince, had a cool pint of another Irish
sat outside and watched the sun set over Margam.

He swallowed what would have been their third date
but couldn't pretend her absence augured well.

The only things they had in common were sex
and a laughably dubious sense of humour.

Both were already wearing thin like the grey pinkness
that leaked skywards over Port Talbot steelworks.

And as he drained the tangible beer he could perceive
that his afternoon hangover would hold its own.

CRYOGENIA
for Angela Carter

He'd bought the largest chest freezer available
so that when she died, he was ready.
He'd put pillows in to make it comfortable
and dressed her in her favourite black nightie.
Shutting the lid he felt consumed with responsibility.

As the days passed he got used to the questions
and friends understood, only too well, that she'd left him.
He would sit and talk to her, sometimes opening the lid
he'd peer in at her skin, so icy-white, so unbidding,
so resistant to his touch, but hers none-the-less.

Occasionally, forgetting the opened lid, he'd drift off
to thirty years ago, among Merthyr Mawr sand dunes
that really hot summer, when he'd first pulled her bra
over her brown, heat dampened breast, caressed it,
pursed his lips to taste the soft salted peanut of her nipple.

Coming round he'd panic to see the melted ice
like a freckle of raindrops on her pale skin.
Slamming the lid shut, he feared her betrayal,
she was in trust to him, there would be no let downs.
He lived in dread of a power-cut, prayed for winter.

Yearning for her, he climbed in and lay with her
but where they touched, though she melted, he froze.
The more impossible it was, the more he wanted her
the more he was tempted by what could never be.
Enticed by her proximity, her nearness woo'd him.

Fingers sticking to her, he lifted her out,
laid her on the living room carpet and kneeled,
noting every change as she languorously defrosted.
Touching the renewed softness of her hair he cried
then put the fire on to warm them both.

They made love by the firelight, him knowing
this couldn't happen again and so, several hours later
having done all he could, he sadly put her back,
switched the fast-freeze button and climbed in.
Entwined in the darkness, his tears became solid.

A MAN CALLED SCHWENK

Entering, Schwenk is illuminating
on the legality of zoophillia
(England and Wales illegal
Nebraska, legal!)
Schwenk is from Nebraska.
A woman once sent me a manuscript
called, 'Schwenk's Lovers'.
The title poem was about a couple
shagging in a university library.
Schwenk is someone you can
easily deny knowing.
Schwenk makes the interloper welcome.
Schwenk doesn't mind anything really.
Schwenk is in love with a buzzing light
he has one in every room he teaches in.
Schwenk has an unidentifiable
Welsh accent.
Schwenk is not Wales's answer
to Roy Orbison, but he could be.
Schwenk is not Greenland
he's more like Rio at Carnival
or at any rate the day after.
Schwenk once sent me a postcard
of a Roman Latrine but only
to illustrate a point about someone.
Schwenk knows nothing is permanent
it's what effect things have that counts
spreading and rippling long after
the thrown stone has plopped.
Schwenk has plopped greatly.
Schwenk creates space for creativity
and then expects you to create
the bastard!
Schwenk would love to suffer

from whiplash.
Schwenk is not just Schwenk
he is, above all else, lovably Norman.
There is no rhyme for Schwenk.

THE BOOKSHOP MANAGER'S FAREWELL

No more
stalking unsuspecting shoplifters.
No more
tie tucked in his trousers.
No more
the no.1 skull
sheening in the striplights.
No more
the purveyor of deviant shelf dividers
and Anglo-Welsh erotica.
No more
mass book writing
because he's nothing else to do
in the small press littered office.
No more
the smooth manipulation
of the passed buck
when the photocopier goes wrong
in the midst of his cut-up concrete epic.
No more
bureaucratic desiderata
inadvertently shifted into cyber limbo.
No more
blamelessness amidst the females.
No more
confronting the vicious man
stealing from the staff room
that led to fundamentalist Tai Chi,
the martial art you do in your slippers.
No more
dealing with that awkward bastard
who always came in at 5.25 pm
to order obscure small press books
that did not exist.

No more
the bulk buying of the
completely unsalable boxed Bob Cobbing.
No more
the unfailingly excellent demonstrations
of how to pack a book so well
no-one would ever be able to unpack it.
No more
the car park space chess game.
No more
the affairs, the non-affairs.
No more
the unrequited cups of coffee.
No more
the irritating stacks of his unsold life.

THE CHAIRMAN'S WALK
i.m. Robin Reeves

Slowly, reluctantly, out of Llandovery
and into the unrehearsed countryside
jumpers and coats tied around waists
a small gaggle of writers plodded.
I was supposed to be in the lead
but it was Robin who knew the way
knew even the driver of the old Alvis
who stopped so they could converse.
Then that laugh, never far away.
It is his laugh I remember the most
rich and sonorously gruff
sparkled with infectious joviality.

Suits he rarely wore, they looked odd on him
but in the oddest jumpers he was at home.
A slightly ruffled, comfortable man
contented with a cigar and a drink
at ease in both languages and landscapes.

Traipsing in the still, late summer heat
beyond where the Roman road ends
in a deeper more natural Wales
he's out of sight, up the green path
but I hear the sound of his laughter
making the country air genial.

COMFORT

From his side's surgically induced holes
protrude tubes the size of garden hoses
which agonize bubbles of blood
with every breath of his single lung.

He painfully trails their analysing boxes
shuffling to the toilet, jerking them behind
face matching his washed-out grey hair.
My father at his worst, struggling not to fade.

Constantly gasping, leaning on the bed's end
persevering in a world with not enough air.
He finally lays back on the mattress, groans.
An anguish of never getting comfortable again.

GREEK

Television brings me Bethany Hughes and ancient Crete.
She presents sea snails, palaces, culture built on purple.
When their civilization was swept away by invaders
the Minoans fled to the Mountains of Mist.
So scared of what or who was below they stayed
for centuries hiding while their world gently crumbled.
Millennia after Minoa had lost everything
Knossos was reborn as a done-up ruin for you
and your fellow tourists to meander around.
You the wandering spirit of the family.

After your email I knew the Minoan's fear.
The decipherment of all 'Linear A' nothing
beside the effect of that one word echoing.
Slowly, very slowly, I cope with it, then I don't.
That one word contains too much modern loss.
From my birth you held me but now it's my turn
as the invader brings your world into hurt.
A tear, a cough, there, there mother. 'Chemo'.

T.B.

I am blowing up my father's left lung.
It is huge and covered in old T.B. scars.
I cannot hyperventilate fast enough
the hole in it burbles deflatingly.
I've got to keep puffing harder and harder
until the doctors can invent micro-surgery.

***   ***   ***

In the 1950's T.B. ward they had enormous pills
that tasted so bad the only way to eat them
was plopped into the morning's sugary porridge.

My father and his fellow patients
are hanging from the top of a door
pulling themselves up to see over it
the man who eats the pills raw
chews them and their papery wrappers
with a relished grim determination.

The other patients go out at weekends
get plastered so bad it counteracts
any good they do being in hospital.
My father is up in the morning
running around the grounds of Sully
in his dressing gown and slippers
keeping fit for his eight-hour shifts.

***   ***   ***

They want to put their eye down his throat
but my father won't let them.
He wants to go home where he's safe,
where he knows he'll be okay.
"They've seen enough of my bloody innards
and I've seen enough of them!"
My mother has started to pray again.

APRIL

While the rains fall in April
my father lies gasping
face in a plastic oxygen mask
that look in his eye
of the non-believer who knows
his time has come to enter oblivion.
There is nothing I can do for this.
Jokes about the afterlife
slipping into another dimension
explanations of quantum mechanics
and the theories of the multiverse
he derides with working-class savvy.

His always black hair
has gone white in just two years.
His face a pallor of grey sky.
I thought he had years left
till, five years ago a coughing fit
collapsed a weakened lung.
A smoker since the late 1930's
and T.B. when young
had left his lungs fibrous.
The doctor prescribed no cure.

Now I sit by his bed
his lips are blue from gasping
constantly unable to get enough
his chest a clogged bellows.
Mum has survived chemotherapy
but he is lost, as am I, listening
to the gurgling rasp of his inhale.

IN THE BACKYARD WITH WALLACE STEVENS

He's resting, in blue and green, on my lap
wondering about unreality's apparent reality
as if the bicycle's disuse was use?

I am in the ordinary elsewhere
watching a small universe of midges
continually disentangle themselves.

Notice the nervous grass snake
caught out in the open
stippled by rose tree shadows

having trouble with the smooth red tiles
energetically meandering
making too little headway.

Pronged flicker kisses rough concrete
and its slooping body straightens train like
glides to the erotic, splayed grass.

Look up at the seductive giant fern
my father planted years ago
in the derelict railway embankment.

Its Indian summer fronds are still green
but a month will turn them crimson
wind raging their flames as no other tree.

Wallace Stevens, left on the chair
is basking, nowhere, in September.
I can only concoct hot coffee.

STRANDED
for Elaine Morgan

We loved the flood
washing over the earth
with cold, clear water
filling our noses with bubbles
allowing our feet to fly.
Down below in the darkness
lurked the slow-moving devil
scouring the sea bed
disgusted with everything.
Up in the light, white and blue
frolicking with evolution
we became longer, smoother
between toes and fingers
stretched frog foot webbing
allowing our souls to dive deeper
but still pull them back
to the air's surface brilliance.
As close as we'll ever come
to the flight of dolphins
to the purity of ignorance
demanded by an aquatic Eden.
Our feeble brains enlargen
to cope with two worlds
the flat one and the other
requiring natatorial movement.
And so when the huge tide
receded before we became ocean
we were left as merely human.

THE BELIEVER'S SOMNAL

Capsizing the catamaran he plummets
underwater, abseiling without a rope.
To his surprise the boat ploughs on
its sails billow with the fulsome current.

Still at the helm, his world has turned about,
heart aquatically slowed, blood flowed to brain
and though there is trouble breathing,
it is no strain more than the usual.

In the sway and heave of the small vessel
the curving sea looks odd, submerged as he is,
waves bulge between ravines whose snaking depths
contort as if time itself were curling.

As he navigates by whale-song, mind evolving,
floating somewhere, awash across sleep and other,
serenely praying to keep adrift, unwoken,
he sends dreams to hail unreachable shores.

Ill at ease, with strange birds swimming by,
above him the ocean's floor rolls with menace
while all under the surface, shining blue light
floods upwards, as if heaven were below.

UNDERWATER
i.m. Marilyn 1951-2011

Slowly she drifts to gentle rest
as a body upon the sea's bed
deep down I am with her
two such strange bottom dwellers.

Her children are in the other room
a surface of sorrow and dried tears
she raised all three on her own
floating debts like paper boats.

I want to make a withering joke
warped with the dark humour
only cynical siblings can share
but she has sunk far too low.

Often alone, I've never felt so lonely
swallowed up by it as we lay here
an ocean's depth pressing over us
air's distant glimmer murkily above.

All should be movement, flow
but it is still, cold and empty.
Too soon I will rise and enter life
to walk dry land drowned by grief.

She witnessed my birth, I her death
her absence is now my companion.
Leaving her there, there are more tears
for all that has been and is yet to come.

TIDE MEMORY

CHARITY CAR PARK

I sit in my car, sunroof open, at the top
of a field's slight incline below which
are an array of automobiles leading down
to the muddy entrance/exit and a hedge
the other side of which is Hay Festival's
angular spread of billowing white canvas.
Huge marquees, banners flapping
like ads for a medieval jousting tournament
but actually filled with book lovers.
To my left a bird is constantly singing.
I watch the slow but steady drift of people
tired and irritable, wandering, searching for their
vehicles which have been misplaced by memory.
Their cars are everywhere but where they left them.
Without signs or row numbers they struggle
life as hard as navigating a field
in casual shoes that aren't country-wise.
The flashing and beeping of their central locking
obscured by sun glare and raucous birdsong.
One obese man, halfway up in breathlessness
slumps exhaustedly against the nearest 4x4
and is rendered apoplectic by its shrieking alarm.
These are the sightseers who are blind to nature.
Even the trees have fairy lights attached so that
in the dark the inept townies don't walk into them.
Amidst all this, the desperate to find their way
cling to the memory of homes, loved ones
the soft comfortable fabric of their journey's end.
Clearly, on this beautiful day, I hear the happy song
of a successful female trilling, "I've found it!"
The only thing the lost have is hope.

WHEN SCAFFOLDERS HOWL

White hard hats just lift or lower the poles and planks
black hard hats have the electric drills in holsters
to untighten the bolts with a brisk parp so clamps
can be dismantled and poles carefully removed.
Years ago they used one manual spanner, wrangled
to hand lever the bolts loose and no hi-viz safety gear
just hard hats and tanned red arms, necks and faces.

The single or double clamps off, they are thrown
into plastic buckets ready to be handed down.
Long poles lowered slowly from man to man
cross poles first, then uprights and wooden planks
all held cautiously with aching arms and shoulders
especially when held over head by hands cold
from the metal even through thick work gloves.
Spilled dust and dirt of planks raised from below
lifting everything up to bring it all down.

From the top they climb, loudly shouting alerts
as, first one side of the building then another
is gradually bereft of its grey iron framework
swinging and clanking along and then lowered
to be finally laid flat on the battered lorry's bed.
There they'll slumber till the next building site
will reverse them back erecting from the ground up
to surround whatever construction requires them.
These yo-yo men will put up and take down
scaffolding for other men to safely work on
for years of constant, consistent steadiness
helping to bring the world we know into being.

These butties are Valley's boys, lilting musical accents
yelping orders, calling warnings, hurling curses
the endless joking, joshing workmates yammering
jibber jabber ribaldry of girls, footie and drinking.

Every scaffolding gang I have ever worked with
will, at some point, tip their heads back and let rip
howling like a wild pack of wolves at a full moon.
Yet at day's end they'll squash into lorries and vans
to travel home weary, thirsty, laughter quieter
till the next morning gathers them together again.

LAVERNOCK POINT

Looking for somewhere to do it
they come across another couple doing it.
Too embarrassed to pass by they shuffle back
to walk in a wide arc from the rocks
to the strands of sand and shale at the sea's edge.

They glance enviously, a hundred yards away,
at the undulating, heat-hazed couple.
His white buttocks thumping, head bobbing,
her brown hands clawing and
her light soles a halo of activity.

Out of view and back at the warm rocks
her cut-off shorts prove momentarily awkward
and the towel doesn't take the roughness
from the rash of barnacles as they'd hoped,
but how delicious the cool, gentle sea-breeze
caressing the hot crack of his arse,
coaxing out her whiskery nipples.

After climaxing in a froth of saltiness
they sit up to see the other couple
walking at the sea's edge, trying to look away.
They laugh raucously and drain the last
of the Californian pink white wine.

They have yet to get bitten by the sandflies
or spot the large sweating man up on the cliffs
crouching behind his digital camcorder.

GOGGLE

Having endured the loneliness
of constantly being left behind
to splutter in their wakes,
at long last he can just about
keep up with the super-fit
gorgeous female swimmers.
Be-goggled he thrashes up the pool
drooling underwater at their
tanned bodies, wetly clad
in drip-dry blue Lycra,
slipping through the liquid
with the ease of the genuinely erotic.

Chasing after, panting and gasping,
he's able to keep up for longer
and is even becoming slimmer.
His crawl is pretty good
but it's his breaststroke
that is really sublime;
though to be super cool he sports
a neat victory roll backstroke.
Butterfly, as everyone knows,
is only for posers.

When the swimming club leave
him floating in the shallows,
he watches those strong women
their movement languid
their hair uncapped,
their arm muscles flexing
as they lift themselves out
in a cascade of slimness.
He hankers with all his lost youth
their poise and jauntiness
as they go to laugh and joke
nakcd in the showers.

BACKROBATICS

In Waterstones January sales I am seduced
by the lower shelves' possibilities.
Straightening up I receive a now familiar spinal stab.
My knees collapse, my eyes roll upwards
and I exasperate a series of loud guttural sighs.
It's a small comfort that at least I know I'm not dying.

People around the sales table move rapidly away
as if I'm calling on Jehovah to damn them all
and they don't want to take any chances.
The security guard reaches for the gun
he doesn't have, but which
he's always imagined he does.
A female assistant,
it's always a woman who does this,
sensibly asks if I'm alright
and if I want an ambulance.
"Bad back," I gasp, "be alright in a minute."

People smile with relief and consolation
and warily edge forward.
I struggle to my feet and then move around
slowly, searching out the pain so as to avoid it,
then to ease and manipulate it.

At odd angles I make my way across the road
to The House of Fraser cosmetics department.
Giving me a wide girth, women buying Givenchy,
Obsession and Chanel are seriously perturbed
by my bar-less limbo arching,
my satanic neck rotations and
my constabulary knee-bends.

Approaching the Patterson's
chocolate-coated shortbreads

I am surrounded by burly walkie-talkies.
A bad attitude here would see me
lobbed out the door to connect
spine first with the paved walkway,
but the humour is universal as I tell them,
"Me back's gone – just gave out in Waterstone's."
Laughing, they leave me to it as I spinally gyrate
and gesticulate with apparent abandon
like a demented tai-chi fanatic
towards china and glassware.

THE RESOLUTIONISTS

By mistakc I go swimming the first week in January.
Slipping in beside the regulars, marooned in the shallows,
we float, exchange capitulatory nods and acknowledge
that we won't be swimming much today
or for the next few weeks because the pool is filled
with the chaos of New Year's resolutionists.
The dumpy, flabby, love-handled ungainliness
of the hopelessly unfit enthusiastically striving
for the unobtainable, instant sleekness.

Non-swimmers are splashing, frantically doggy-paddling,
disregarding the length lanes to swim widths,
unable to see because they don't have goggles,
colliding catastrophically with the backstrokers
then surfacing like fountains with flushing pink faces
after hilariously trying to breathe underwater.

Much worse than those are they who
years ago used to swim and dive with prowess
but haven't seen water since and yet insist
that ten or twenty years makes no difference.
And so we see them, these lucky ones,
triple-back-flipping off top with aplomb,
sprinting up the pool like Olympic Tarzans,
not realising the cost of their over-exertions,
tomorrow's seized muscles, the inability to get out of bed
or the ambulance trip to hospital for emergency traction.

And then consider the unlucky ones
who without a moment's reprieve are reminded
half a length down the pool by breathlessness,
cramps, heart attacks or just plain drowning.
Their awkward bodies cast up poolside
and, embarrassingly, through coughs and vomit,
revived, ringing in their ears the news,
"You're alive, but just a bit too old!"

Up the deep end at the macho springboards
the incomplete somersault's smacked back of the skull
or the man sprawled in a stupor, having mis-bounced
and gone head first into the tiles. He missed the water!
And, from the roof high, top board, the glorious bellyfloppers
are stinging themselves scarlet with a smashing slap.

The next to worst of all these is the man
who plummeted into the lane divider
and neatly garrotted himself on the wire
between the sharp plastic floats.

The very worst, we all agree, is the poor sod
who jumped off top to hit one foot either side
of the lane divider's plastic teeth and wire.
Unlike the garrotted man he was alive to suffer.
Bright purple in his agony, hands clamped on genitals,
rigidly foetal, almost unbearable to look at
as he was dragged out and put on the stretcher
sideways because he wouldn't go flat.

Ever alert to the danger surrounding us
we regulars swim slowly through the carnage
carefully avoiding collisions or even contact
like ghosts in an aquatic movie by Hieronymus Bosch.

Back at the shallow end's comparative safety
we guesstimate that by February this will be over
when the resolutionists, who do it to get healthy,
in the hope of living longer, have all inflicted
injuries or done permanent damage or just died.
Few survive as swimmers. One may become a regular,
although this is extremely rare, but until then
the ambulances are lined up outside like fire engines.

THE LAST SWIM IN EMPIRE

Today he has swum the last big 50.
He has the pleasant, tired looseness
the after-swim ease of everything
as if he were still in water
floating through the blue
gently covered in coolness
as the gliding plash of the overarm
noses into the whispering rush.
The regulars had parted affirming
"Last day in the old pool, first day in the new"
with all the mock certitude of a large rock
slumbering down to a murky ocean floor.
From that downward wending escapes
the minute bubble that is Wales.
How long will it take to emerge
in a splutter of unintelligible linguistics
as its air becomes everywhere else.

Perhaps his thirty years of afternoon swims
will return him to play in Cardiff's bay,
all silted, choked and barraged, where
as a child he laughed through ships' wakes
with a pat of butter hidden under a flat stone
to rub off black oil stains from wet skins.
Now, being much more accomplished in water,
he'll swim out through the Bristol Channel,
into the Irish Sea and, oblivious of the pollution,
will slap every wave with the energy
of the new-born enthusiast.
Carousing with dolphins,
splashing curious seagulls
and shadow boxing nervous sharks,
water rapturously gurgles beneath
as his body reaches for movement and air.

The sensual mile or so of depth below
just a breath of mist on the earth's mirror.
With all tiredness hours away,
the challenge of an unused body
between the bright blue and the dark green,
a speck sandwiched by two atmospheres,
he knows, like all the creatures,
languages and cultures of the sea,
that to swim is everything.

TIDE MEMORY

1.

The tide is just a memory.
I stand here, where The Red House
used to be, where apartment blocks
and fencing keep us from the sea,
and through galvanised wires I gaze
looking at conformity, a bland expanse
of gently rippled, level grey water
and try to conjure up the bay
as it was before the becalming barrage;
tide out, wet dunes of slick mud
solid waves of abandoned boats
that mesmeric ever-changing quality
of light reflected, desolate beauty.
For a moment it is vividly there
then, like blown smoke, it's gone.

2.

The tide is just a memory
but its lulling pull still has effect
drawing you now beyond the barrage
to where the sea still has the rhythm
the slow heart beat the city has lost,
to where muck is just visible beneath
the monstrous landscaped rocks.
There's talk now of filling in the bay
developers want it all cement, plastic
or glass sculpted and modernistic
into a Disneyesque theme park,
one up on Barry Island at last.

3.

The tide is just a memory
it is all progress so they tell us.
Such soap opera lies you've got to laugh
botch jobs, peeling paint's what we got
profit margins increase, quality decreases
unaffordable houses, swanking offices
separated by the old Butetown railway
a dim stone brick-blocked embankment
keeping the Wharfites from Tiger Bay
an economic apartheid splitting the docks
whose inhabitants are being priced out
no doubt, when they've been got rid of,
'redevelopment' will also start there
finally eradicating the dark community.

4.

The tide is just a memory
as I look across the bloated bay
at the barrage and motorway bridge
all before me is water like soup
boats churning, spinnakers billowing
pillocks pretending to sail the seven seas
while locals' boats, once moored free
on the Taff's banks, are all gone now
the marina's quickly put a stop to that.
For the few months it's sunny
I can almost kid myself it's better
till the sluicing rains and bitter winds
wash away all the sun kissed promises
as Cardiff ceases to ape California.
The planner's paradise missed the mark
they got the weather wrong for a start.

5.

The tide is just a memory.
I can't help wonder why they did this?
Was it just for convenience sake?
So some can go boating and sailing
whenever their carefree wishes want?
Anaesthetized from any sense of ocean
time and tide eradicated by egotism
worth more than the bay's ecology
or the opinions of many that live here.
Fields I rode ponies on are factories
Grange Moor smells still of garbage
gasses burping, fishless mutated pond scum
things gradually shifting, trickles seeping
from small drops landslides may grow.

6.

The tide is just a memory
only to be seen in art gallery photographs
showing the true beauty of the old bay
nearly always pictures with the tide out
of a time when you could glance up
every hour or so and the whole panorama
had changed from mud slurried or cracked,
tilted masts, buoys askance, chains curled,
water refracting light to fill or empty
the optic nerve's myriad cadences
washing the bay and the senses clear
like tidal lungfuls of fresh salty air.
Now there's midges, stagnation and asthma
a paddling pond for yuppiedom incarnate
still oozing the glossy, plastic dream
'Hollywood glitz comes to Grangetown'
while in the suburbs tumble weeds roll.

7.

The tide is just a memory
much like the multi-billion pound quango
that paid architects, planners, contractors
to suck up their payments then move on
leaving my city in pollution's sorry grasp
the ghosts of dead birds, rotting fish
haunting our infamous seaside resort
celebrated for its complete lack of a beach.
Outsiders creamed off the top-cat jobs
while locals cram call centres and services
waiting hand and foot or selling bullshit
living full time on part-time salaries
as the homeless cope with improved
suicide rates and a rising crime rate
caused by people so bored they thieve
for needing what TV cannot soothe
do violence just to see if they're alive.

8.

The tide is just a memory
now the silted-up bay is perfectly dull
Cardiff has become a cosmetic mud pack
packaged jobs created for hype addicts
desperately pushing the laundered buck
buying and selling a thousand times over
a third-rate American dream never realised
fobbed off by pots of brass at rainbow's end.
What those hoardings predicted in 1992?
Mostly nice white middle-classness in sunshine
where blacks proliferate in 38% unemployment.
Nothing is ever as good as advertised but
still we live in the shortfalls between
the sheen of paint and the wood where
the grubby grabby money men fear to tread.

9.

The tide is just a memory
but still there's some good old mud
albeit slumped lonely on the banks
only to be reached by squeezing through
chain link fencing or between buildings
where you're warned you're not supposed to go
but children always find a way to defy rules
to play no matter the stink and the pollution
because where there is muck there is fun
no Waders now just worms and mud pies
sliding the sliminess, making dodgy rafts
swimming in the oily Taff, I did that
just a nipper not even into double figures.
Whatever mess is made of our bay
to kids it's home, something to cling to.

10.

The tide is just a memory
how I miss it now it's gone
only the Bay of Fundy, Nova Scotia
in all the world had a greater rise and fall.
The sea's winding, inevitable ebb and flow
both brought and took away, as life does
but now Cardiff's flowing pulse has stopped
and I am at the water's edge waiting for it
to start and knowing it won't so I suck it up
move on, cities are always changing
demolishing, building something we love
or hate or simply couldn't care less about.
We'll use the good, ignore the bad
and by living here make it our own.
Cycling across the barrage I meet my old self
the tideless greets the tidal and we stare
across two different waters
to slowly acknowledge that
the tide is just a memory.

WINTER CYCLING

WINTER CYCLING

A wrapped-up rain proof ninja
I wheel my steel steed outside
mount it under soldered grey sky.
Bolt on back light, clipped on front,
pedals perambulate into the snow,
wind-rip bite waters uncovered eyes,
chest breath chill factor tightened,
face and hands sleet seared, icy raw,
shining the way my bright-red nose.
Hard pumping legs slowly warming
the inner body furnace radiates
till the nipping sting isn't so noticeable.
Fat heavy treaded tyres slide skid
warily churning powdered road,
trucks wheel slicks, runnelled, sluicing,
long fording gutter filled hail slush.
I glide, slicing into shivery crispness,
car headlights enhancing the lucid mist
hover dusted with white frosting,
half rain, half snow's fleecy drizzle
some sticks to me, some melts, soaks in.
I ride this frozen world grit lit and grim.

URBAN BLESSINGS

May your breakfast always be aromatic
May your car never get soggy
May rainwater always be deflected
May your house never sneeze
May cigarettes always exhale you
May your unemployment payment never go on holiday
May smog always enhance your mystery
May your shoes never wallow in dogshit
May friends always go along with the whoppers you tell
May your salt shaker's lid never be unscrewed
May your arguments always be boisterous
May your partner never wear the wrong clothes
May your haircuts always have a sense of humour
May serrated paper never fail to rip for you
May your optician always be acute
May you never score a hat-trick of own goals
May you always be sober when pulled over
May you never have enough regrets to fill your old age
May you always see beauty in street lights
May you still be drunk in the morning

KAPUT

Aerial and electric unplugged
I sit and stare at the blank, undusted screen.
The back unscrewed, resting on its side,
revealing circuit boards and the menacing tube.
All lifeless now or so pronounced
by the TV repairman, who last fixed it ten years ago,
who, broken video under arm, signs its death certificate
with a screwdriver's bluntness.

Twenty-five years is a good span for a TV.
Not like losing a loved one but a pet dog maybe.
It will, however, be missed more than either,
providing nothing now to fill up the loneliness,
to chatter and engage blandly by deceit.

Through the silence at supper time
I can hear the gorgeous black girl next door
singing beautifully out of tune with her dog,
who howls along like the static after close-down.
Faint but audible, muffled by the wall,
in the background of their duet, yes, she's left her TV on.
A flicker in her corner I'm blind to, with the sound
turned down, but not quite enough.

CONSERVATORY

A few dull sporadic taps on the roof's
transparent corrugated plastic sheeting
like something dropping small stones
the taps increase slowly, then rapidly
until it is a recognisable downpour.
I have listened to it most of my life.
Once it was panes of glass showing
moving cloud sky squares I looked at
as a small boy visiting Grampy Joe.

As a young man I helped my father
replace sepia-tarnished glass for plastic.
Bright clear light filling the kitchen
Grampy Joe marvelled at the heavens.
He died just four years later aged 94.

The plastic fatigued, faded to opaque
cracked it made gloom, increased drips
till ten years ago I elbowed dampness
replaced it all, brought dry brilliance
back to an old kitchen in poor shape.

Now I sit drinking coffee, staring up
at the blue grey steady drizzle blurring
cloud clarity, distorting transparency
a hearing of its heavy downfall patter
as water clatters the kitchen drum skin.
I remain dry in spite of wind hurl
buffeting spray hiss and gurgled roar
flash flowing downpipes, swirling gutters
weather's cacophonous liquid symphony
closes with a smattering of light droplets
gently surfacing sound to clear blueness.

PLAYA ESPAÑA

The sand is burning, acres of it,
dredged and put here by the megaton,
50 yards out and the warm water
is still only waist high.
This is the sea turned into a resort
all blow-up boats, surfboards and balls
squealing kids out screaming the gulls
where the slim and the tanned can
cavort safely in an aquatic playground .

Up to my shoulders
coldness at my ankles
I put on shaded goggles
and kick out, the sea bed
disappearing beneath me.
Trying to dive is hard work.
I never get used to how difficult
it is to sink in the sea.
In a swimming pool's light water
you can easily glide under the surface
but here a full stroke is needed
just to keep you submerged.
Powering down to the murkiness
along the bottom, further, deeper,
there is a depth at which you'll stay
the pressure negating buoyancy.
Then you can float in a hinterworld
of solitude amidst the jungle deeps
where predators still rule
where you confront yourself
and know that you are just
some creature's mid-day snack.

Surfacing, I swim on,
to a man-made reef of rocks.
Swaying I stand up, waist high
out of the waves and look back
at humanity dipping its toes in
staying where it's safe and warm.
I turn and look out to sea
wonder what further depths
and revelations are out there
waiting beyond everything.
Soon I'll have to move but
suddenly I'm not so sure
which way to swim.

MARINARO DIABOLICAL

Above El Campello harbour the next table
has adventurously ordered sea spiders.
We watch the waiter place the plate down
upon it something from a science fiction film.
The consternation on the couple's faces
is only too evident as they try to act
as if this was exactly what they wanted
in fact, what they are looking forward to
and will relish with lip-smacking and wine.
To everyone else it is obvious they either
didn't understand the menu or convinced
themselves it was a culinary concoction's
fancy name and not, as it is, a real spikey
legged, deep sea spider, monstrously large
covering the whole plate and replete with
gooey, slime-filled abdomen and salad.

NEPTUNE ON DAYTIME TV

He slews across the lurid set
contemptuously drunk, almost incapable
but blasé with how far he's sunk.

Once he was an idol and then
some bastard invented navigation
and maps ruled him out.

Washed up he still looks good
tanned, moisturized, nipped and tucked,
his ancient age unfathomable.

The host asks what he's called,
Neptune or Poseidon? Nep smiles
raises an eyebrow like a boat prow.

"I have as many names as there are fish
but Neptune's okay, gotta love that Latin,
great singers and even greater food."

The host asks what he does now?
Neptune smiles a barrier reef, slurs
"Try to avoid all your mess." He drinks.

"I let you parasites into my home
and you've just trashed it, there's little
I can now do for my fabulous aquatics.

I was worshipped once, libations poured
now it's just take, take, take, and no give."
Nep drinks, submerges into himself.

The host points at Nep's tipple and asks
if more liquid is required. Nep swirls
"An empty glass is an unhappy glass!"

Cutting over the applause, the host asks
what happened to his trident? "Left it in
a watering hole?" Nep waves dismissively.

"Someone's probably using it as a toasting fork."
Giggles ripple, old Nep drinks some more.
"Big toast!" quips the host to gales of laughter.

Attempting edginess mixed with bile
the host asks if he still wrecks ships?
"Johnny boy, I never wrecked ships!"

Nep shudders like breakers falling,
"Why blame me for your incompetence?
You humans with your shallow self-interest."

He grimaces, eyes glaring, summons up a drop
of the oceanic greatness he once commanded,
"A shrug of my shoulders and I could drown you all."

Neptune gulps wine, grins like an attacking shark.
The audience, secretly thrilled, laugh nervously
feeling the massive pull of his undertow.

The host, oozing smarm and apprehension,
feeling the fear and losing his nerve, smiles
"Could you really still do that?" Neptune squalls.

His deep voice tsunamies into the camera,
"I gave life to this earth, I can take it back easy."
Knocks his glass over. "All I'd have to do is dry out."

THE MODERN POET'S FETISH FOR A MAP POEM

Philip's Mercantile Marine
Atlas of the World, 1904.
He opens it at the equator
huge pages, card thick,
their edges worn soft and floury.
Charting oceans with equal importance
to the multi-coloured lands
it would have been splayed
on the bridge of some ship
loaded with phosphorus
nudging small icebergs
through the Magellan Strait.

He rips the pages out carefully
lays them flat, 20 by 30 inches,
the seven seas across his floor.
Placing his body patterns over them
his West German scissors start to cut
and all the cartography bends and shifts,
tectonic plates cavorting
into a warped, unknown planet.

Folding and sewing he joins new worlds.
Pacific and Atlantic back-to-back,
the coasts of China and Japan merging
with Europe, Scandinavia and Russia.
His feet become icy Poles apart,
the Americas span his mid-drift,
Australia a skew-whiff corkless hat,
Africa and India his sturdy legs.
On a whim he uses the leftover U.K.
for a big knotted wide-boy tie.

At the local pub, wearing geography,
his Earth carouses in like the wind,

shimmers in a Black Sea of liquor,
Karaokes the scorched wildernesses
till he ruffles out, a looming storm cloud
to the nearest disco's mirrored globe
below which his paper planet will twirl.

Hat floating off the sweaty edge,
his latitude gyrating longitude,
his jacket full of hurricanes,
his trousers full of tidal waves
till his torrential drinking
drains the Dead Sea and his Poles
global warm him to the street
where earthquakes shift his axis,
he head-butts the man in the moon
and his orbit collides with the gutter.
There his molten stomach erupts
and his tie suffers devolution.

He lays moaning like the Himalayas.
Jacket and trousers totally tornadoed
their continents awaiting the ridge
of low pressure from the North
whose rain will gently
wash him mapless.

SENEDD
for John Osmond

This shirt had never been worn.
Bought new several years ago
there was a dispute about where it came from
so it was shoved in the back of a cupboard.

And there it stayed, crumpled, folded all wrong
till some men, rummaging through our house
came across it still in its cellophane.
We weakly admitted it was ours.

After a debate and some argy-bargy
they agreed that we could have the shirt
as long as the cellophane wrapper was theirs.
They seemed delighted. So were we.

Dust-laden it looked faded, fatally creased
but the twin-tub soon swirled it clean
and, rinsed out, it dripped its age away
flapped on the line, played tricks with the wind.

This shirt, that for far too long
had smelt musty, of worms and old damp
suddenly came up dry, bright and crisp
smelling of sunshine and ammonia.

The ironing board's awkward legs
propped it against the hot, flat iron
which smoothed it wrinkle free
showed its elegant, snug quality.

Wearing it freshly washed and ironed
the shirt felt both cool and warm
a distinction peculiarly Welsh.
We knew it was ours then.

SANCTUARY

They'd been told to go home
so he was sat in his car
in the early November dusk,
rain rumbling on the roof,
Jackie Wilson's 'Danny Boy'
cascading from the stereo,
the windows clear because
he'd sprayed them with anti-mister.

Site abandoned, the manager stands
in the Portakabin doorway, fag hand aglow.
Inside the car the wooden steering wheel
holds his scratch-covered hands,
still not used to the harshness expected.
In the base of his seat, his spine
lets him know it'll be a while yet
before he's used to the lifting,
the mornings or the yoga of slating.

Tomorrow would find him here again
laughing as they used the crane
to move the Portakabin without
telling the manager who'd
think it had been lifted.

For now though, he needs this moment,
to sink back into himself,
to just listen,
before he turns the ignition
and lights the luminous green
under the sixties dashboard cowling,
before everything starts happening again
after the song's last, unbelievable note.

SLATE RIPPER

Slipping the ripper's tongue
a dark worn metal snake sliver
under the old broken slate
the long double-headed sword
slides in to viciously hook nails.
Hammered, they are yanked out
and the matt-black fragments
clatter and tumble down slope
to nestle in the gutterpipe.
An inch-wide strip of pliable
lead nailed in the tooth gap
the replacement slate smoothly
shoved upwards to alignment
and the soft metal is easily bent
over with the gentlest of taps.
Blowtorch the lead strip's end
till it melts and solidly welds
to centre the brittle rectangle
holding it firmly in place.
Then move on to the next
shattered, cracked or holed
slate needing to be removed
by the slicked French kiss
of this flat steel phallus.

'FULL HOUSE'

The four of us sat on the roof's sunny side
having a break, rolling our own,
the breeze scattering tobacco
and conversation across new slates.

She appeared in the big window next door.
Began tossing her clothes off without a care,
oblivious to the four of us opposite, enraptured,
undrawn smoke curling over our fingers.

Bra and panties abandoned with a flick and a kick
as we nudged and smirked at her glorious 'Full House'.
She cavorted, pinched her flesh, viewed her mirrored rear
until she glanced out and saw us sat there, gawping.

Mouth an exclamation, her litheness first froze
then panicked and leapt her into the wardrobe
slamming its slim door shut behind her.
We nearly fell off the roof with laughter.

We watched the wardrobe angrily shaking
as, locked in, she banged and shouted and just might
have been there all day but for her man, who rushed in.
Let out she pointed, from his arms, but we'd scarpered.

SWOOSH

This sea of rooves, wind lashed
proof against the heaven's onslaught
cloudmass roaming, tilting rain
all water sloughed into valleys
guttered to pipes and drained.
Slates glisten, shining in heat
roll, drip and lift, an ocean's solid swell.
Ponder here, clambered over and scaffolded
to tar, nail and saw rough wood,
a life unvarnished, swaying, adrift
miles of them under endless skies.
Crest of a roof, legs astride a different world
light men, feathered, nimble footed,
they sail these rectangles like smoke
leaving no trace when gone but newness.
To work on rooves is to love the horizon
to realize that most city people live in holes
with only cut-up slices of blue or grey
trapped by civilisation, their world blinkered,
they need to travel to achieve for a moment
vastness and with it the eternal like the sea.
Coming down, roofers have to re-adjust
forget what is up there, all that light,
stoop into shadows, talk a lesser language.
Learn how to interact with ordinary people,
who have forgotten, hold it in till the morning
when the ladder rungs beckon and 'up top'
they can at last get a good lungful.
To feel at home up here, where the worst thing
would be to fall back down
to where you don't belong.

THE HAND

The look of it was strange to him.
He'd worked all day to felt and batten
both sides of the roof before it rained
and now, sat on the crest, the hammer silent,
he raised his right hand and remarked it.
The pure grey light gave it clarity
an astonishing quality of visibleness
as if it were more than visible
in the tension before the downpour.
He could smell diesel from the street,
taste iron from the railway lines
and see the coming rain fall
on houses half a mile away.
Turning his hand he studied
the blackening scar tissue of grazed knuckles,
the chipped nails and thick veins.
Turning it back, the dirt had fingerprinted
his whole palm with dust and memory.
How many moments before this
had he stopped and felt it all move on?
Smoke altered direction from chimneys,
litter scratchily changed its mind
and he tracked the wind's effects
moving things toward him along the street
like a wall of invisibleness happening.
As it hit him the first cold drops
tapped his flat upraised palm.
He would never come down from this.

THE ORMOND ESTATE

Ice wind whipping over the crest
ears bright purple, head unblessed,
cutting the brick in the chimney stack
for lead to be fitted front and back.

Everything damp, the roof and the tools
and at every hammer tap the gale howls.
The valleys are all done, how he longs to go
to sit in his chair by the gas fire's glow.

But stuck up here now, wind up his back
bending lead he can hear his joints crack.
When that is done he slates the last slates,
overlapped to the top, him and two mates.

Then the coldest at the roof's apex
they finally finish by cementing the crest.
The sky is ominous as they untie the ropes
slide thin ladders awkwardly over dark slopes.

Slip the rubbish down the scaffolding chute,
the tools are thrown in his old car boot.
Ladders aloft their van, they laugh and joke
about brass monkeys, gasp a last smoke.

When they leave he looks up at the roof,
the last of thirty-two houses made rain proof,
but soon to have a family, a welcome mat.
In years to come he'll point and say; "I did that."

WALKABOUT

Hearing the front door quietly click shut
he lurches awake, staggers up, out of bed
into slip-on shoes, grabs glasses, keys and coat
and runs to see her several houses down.

Mid-winter, middle of the night, breath
billowing icy white, his mother's in a hurry
to see her parents who died thirty years ago
happily wearing just slippers and night gown.

Running after her the large man's coat flaps
in the freezing wind. Catching up he pleads, argues
and cajoles with to come back to her home
but she's not having any of it in spite of the cold.

So out of place they look a passing police car
pulls over for names, addresses and suspicion.
With the dawning realisation of how far gone she is
the smiling constabulary get her to give in.

He thanks them at the front door as she feels
the radiator's warmth and then treads softly
up the familiar stairs to forget all till next time.
He lies awake praying she's asleep and waiting.

MADOC AT THE JOBCENTRE

Told them I was a sailor, vast experience
first man to cross the Atlantic and all that
but would they listen, no, didn't want to know.
They said a computer course was the thing
that it would make an administrator out of me.
"I can't do that," I said "I'm a prince of the sea."
I tried to explain the stars, the smells of the wind
the way tides shift, how to use a sextant.
They only wanted to talk flat-earth bullshit.
Well I smiled and went along so far
I needed the money and I'm practical enough
but you can only take so much crap
before you reverse their shrinking universe
berating them with expansion, the ever-increasing
hungry and homelessness where chaos theory
is rampant and nowhere is everywhere.
Money and food are ceasing to exist and life
is unravelling into another dimension.
Shelter there is but it's fading faster than twilight.
The utter pointlessness of their rules
when worlds are spinning apart and honesty
is what will get you kicked off the dole
so fast they'll want you to return
the payments they have yet to send you.

None of this is new to me, soon you'll know.
The joy of being completely alone doesn't last.
You think it's plain sailing, future assured
horizon keenly acknowledged by Sat Nav?
That's just when you'll hear the water's roar
as the boat tips over your world's edge
and when you are floundering overboard
the welfare state won't save you,
New Deal torpedoed that one.

When everyone is homeless, you just know
they'll close the Job Centres. You poor sods
you'll be more lost at sea than ever I was.
Like Icarus, treading water, upside down,
flight wings pulling you under.
Even then you'll find rock bottom
further down than you think!

NO PARKING PLEASE

Taking the ball-pate hammer
to the red Japanese hatchback
blocking his garage doors
wasn't the right thing to do.
It was not reasonable backlash.

But the windows, lights and mirrors
exploded so deliciously
he couldn't resist, hypnotized
by his own outlandish frenzy.
His hammer's wild staccato
bulleted the wings
pockmarked the bonnet
and corrugated the roof.

Zeal had him back in the garage
searching for the one sharp chisel
to slash the bastard's radials
and go completely punk
on the plush car seats.

Sweating, mouth gobbing white air,
he staggered back in awe
looked around the deserted lane.
The demolished red Japanese hatchback
scrapped alfresco
its glass spilt like sugar
a work of art without applause.

Twenty minutes later
sat on a bus in the warm, he picked
broken glass from his boot tread
and smugly imagined the owner's
frustrated disbelief when he discovered
his car, like his ego, suddenly shattered.

POGO

Before the Mosh Pit or Thrash
way before all of that
as a young teen I Pogo'd
in the sweat spit thrall of Punk.
From my cropped spikey red hair
to my bright-red patent D.M.'s
I gave myself completely
to the splenetic raw energy.
Young and iridescent
as strobe lighting
the frenetic kinesis of rhythm
the abandon of body to the beat
the twisted Clash euphoria
which would live with me
across the daunting years
till hearing it again
in hopeless middle-age
part in humour, part for the thrill
I Pogo'd once more.
As others laughed
I became again
the fearless teenager
not caring what others thought
till after a joyous upward bounce
my Achilles tendon twanged
and I careened floorwards.
Forcing myself up in grim embarrassment
I slipped back, hitting the elbow's funny bone
and, giving in to pain and gravity
I sprawled there, Spasm dancing
almost in time to the music.

FRIENDSHIP

She watches the mouse in his kitchen
her one eye buried in the bed's pillow.
Through the door she sees it creep
across the Formica and into the microwave,
its door left open in his hurry to leave.
His bed smells of him, biscuity.
Her mess of tangled red hair
that had flowed over him
was now annoying her.
Ever since the break up
weird shit like this happened.
She fancied him and knew
that sooner or later she'd
have ended up here, but not now.
So completely not now!

The mouse was in the microwave.
She leant over the bed's edge
clawed a silver Reebok and flung it.
The door slammed with the impact.
She got up, looked at the frightened thing
hunched in the corner, then sniffing
all round as if there was some way out.
After toast, coffee and qualms,
she turned the white knob to 10 mins
with the setting at max and thought
it would just be like cooking meat.

The mouse, frantically expands
as the gasses erupt from the inside.
Flesh blistered, bubbled and finally exploded
leaving a red and blackening
withered frame wafting its smell
through the vent to permeate.
She left the note on his table

where he was sure to find it,
"Dear Topher
    dinner is in the microwave!"

LAUGHTER

Terry had slicked-back hair during the Beatles mop-top era and wore check shirts and jeans. Old cine films speckle him working with my father on church rooves, hanging from ropes halfway up the spire. As kids exploring, we'd climb through hatchway after hatchway, roof after roof, liking the complexity of the slated maze, stunned by the blue skies, the dizzying look down. Thrown over the edge and lowered by orange rope to Terry, we were grizzling with fear. My father laughing, knowing it was safer than letting us on ladders with rungs too far apart for our legs. There we were, dangling but secured by his unfathomable knots.

Years later, when I'd become Terry, who'd disappeared into our history, I could never do knots like my dad's, which held firm till one strand was tugged and the whole thing unravelled so easily, leaving him joking and laughing at mine which had to be unpicked. Once though, forgetting to loop the front of some plaster boards on his van's roof, he pulled up sharpish at a junction and the whole lot slid off and floated, hovercrafting into the intersection's centre. We both dived out, leaving the doors open, waving at the halted traffic whose drivers hooted and laughed as we careened about grabbing boards and chucking them up onto the old van's dented roof.

After tying them down, this time, so firmly you could have picked the van up by them, we leapt in and cautiously drove off, adrenalin mixing with laughter. He regaled me with tales of similar events; boards sailing up in the air at high speed or left in a slather like a deck of spread cards or the bath that had slipped out the back because the doors on that van didn't shut right.

Once, my father, as a boy, and his father had been driving along the then deserted A48. Coming down a big hill at a fair old clip my grandfather had pointed out to my father, "Look at that boy, someone's lost a wheel!" They laughed as it passed them on the inside and wondered which fools it could have happened to, till their car hit the flat and the back hit the road. As my grandfather wrestled the car to the verge my father watched the wheel bounce over it further on. He was sent to get it as his father got the jacks out and swore at the garage which hadn't tightened any of the nuts on that wheel.

Over the verge my father saw it had hit at high speed and completely demolished a farmer's ancient shed. He retrieved the wheel and was breathlessly toiling it up the embankment when he heard, "WHAT THE BLOODY HELL? OY YOU!" He turned and saw a man with a stick and a dog.

Back at the car a nut had been gleaned from every wheel, making three for each including the wheel flopped down as, gasping with irritation my dad told his dad. His dad spun the nuts on rapid like, wound down the jack, slung it in the boot and they leapt in and gave the car full throttle.

As my father and his father had laughed at it, so my father and I laugh at it and though I'd heard the story before from Gramp, my father adds the extra bit to make it his; that as their car crested the rise of the next hill my father, looking back, saw the farmer crest the rise of the verge and look left when it was obvious he should have looked right. Before he could do so, the car dipped out of sight leaving my father eternally puzzled but happy.

Playing ball in the park with Terry, my brothers and I challenged him, "How high can you throw it? Show us." So he did, hurling it out of sight, straight up and to our amazement, it never came down. We hunted for it, searched the park and Terry but it was never to be seen again. Now I know it must have been a trick that, like the farmer, we'd looked the wrong way at just the right moment and Terry had got away with it, left us dangling up there with the ball, a mystery none of us forgot or failed to believe in, in spite of my father's incredulous, raucous laughter.

MARGAM PARK

After the failed job interview I was let in free
and so wandered up to see the Celtic crosses
names of old chieftains, saints, princes and kings
of the Dark Ages when every village had a lord
every town and city had a prince or king.
In those wondrous times before the English
invaded; raping, pillaging, slaughtering
stealing our land, the worst kind of immigrant.

Leaving the building I walk the grounds
through arrayed statues and sculptures
and into shaded lushness of green forest.
April sun dappling the light into flickers
the soft wet, earthy plant smells sinking
my mind through time to hear water rivulating
rustling near, suddenly louder, then too loud
a strange, unfamiliar multi-pattering surrounds
solidifies me as, from beyond into the here
all around a herd of deer comes to a stand still.
Nibbling leaves and grass, stags, bucks, does
and very young fawns are with me, this moment
mesmerically in their midst, rapturously honoured
motionless as a gravestone, stunned by splendour.
An elder head goes up, turns, blinks, and as one
they run, a river of hooves flowing away into
the unknowable and sussureal forest leaving
this man cut adrift, awed by nature, lifted.

FOX ON THE ROOF

Late Monday night reading Canadian
Al Purdy's, 'Red Fox On Highway 500'
of him seeing a fox near midnight
running along the road ahead of his car
a truly majestic bedtime poem.

I have seen red foxes in the lane
at the back of my urban house
cunning opportunistic raiders
of our delicious garbage put out
late Monday nights for Tuesdays.

Early next morning, sipping tea
I look up and see a red fox perched
on top of my lean-to conservatory roof
slunk against the red house wall
then nosing about like a prowler.

I stare at it mesmerised till it moves
down to the valley and out of sight.
I rush to window to see the fox's red tail
jump down to the wall and disappear
into my massively overgrown garden.

I sit and contemplate the red fox
that smallish gap in my lane door
just big enough to squeeze through
for a regular dustbin man's holiday
in its swanky, inner-city lad pad.

The fox has had good hunting here
birds, rats and maybe that squirrel
I once saw up by the chimney before
it ran down the roof to the wall's ivy
another red bushy tail disappearing.

What life is this? My garden full of it
thriving amidst the trees and bushes
these past few years I've seen more
birds and bees than ever clinging
to the brambles, lilac trees, roses etc.

I realize that what was wanted is a space
just a tiny fragment of back-yard wilderness
left to its own resources and miraculously
these almost forgotten creatures re-appear
that, like anything, all they need is a chance.

REEMAAAARRKAAABUL
(uh Kaairrdiff lullaabi)

Bedtiem 'Jaabberwocky'
sendin duh Saandmaan
tuh clowz lidul uzzuks iez
wid staardust sprinkul

tuh fli sleep intuh dreem
beefower dyh ate o clok
monstur prowels duh laandin
sniffin owt duh waykful

redee tuh drink duh blud
uh duh refewgees uv nod
so if yoos bee preetendin
faaik it flaabertaaastikaly

bee comaa ded tuh dis wirld
aan duh neksd, paancaaik flaat
coopeed in duh caasul dunjun
in duh deepist minds mien

waandrin paast Laarnog Poyunt
aarn dowun bee trikd bi im
tikin liek graampees waatch
liek ees gor uh faairee storee

aaskin aakword kwestuns
liek Klaaarksee or Paaarksee?
(dats aalwayz aal aakordin)
Baazzee Ieelund or Aaaleekaantee?

keep yuh gorpurs shut tiet
if is golum tung raasps yuh tows
doh ir tikuls dowun daair skwirm
jes fink uv eetin cheeez on towsd

aarn wen ut laasd ee uv skaarpurrd
yoo kaan waarmlee snugul dowun
tuh sleep duh widee snooozez
dreem uv pit pownees praancin

raaaftin on duh river Taaaf
bee em eks bunee opin duh baaraaj
skofin Dorofees orf duh bone
kuryd chiken an lowdsa chips

levitayt frum Caarolien street baak
tuh duh graaing end wid tumee ful
yoo wul kip til mornin fiends yoo
dedo an snorin sumting maaavelus!

NOTES

APRON

Before wireless mobile phones, all phones were what is now quaintly known as 'landlines'. There was only one phone to a house and it was nearly always in the hallway. For a working-class home to have two phones would have been considered outrageous. At my mum's insistence my dad had an extension put into the kitchen.

NOT WAVING BUT CAPSIZING

My father's dinghy was a 'Solo'. It had boxed-in air compartments which made it unsinkable. Because of their large flat top, this made the gunwales much more comfortable to sit on than most dinghies. I have been told that they are now considered to be an 'old man's' dinghy.

BROGUES, CIRCA 1971

Cardiff Central bus station used to be in a large space in front of Cardiff Central railway station. The red double-decker buses in those days had no doors just an opening in the back left-hand corner so they could be jumped onto and off of if needed.

NEVUH FUHGET YUH KAAIRDIFF

Fraank Fanaarkaapaan – This was based on a radio character called Fred Fanakapan that my dad and other Cardiffians used to use to call someone they didn't know or couldn't remember the name of. (Oi, Fanakapan, come over here a minute!) I changed the Fred to Frank in honour of Frank Hennessy who founded The Cardiff Language Society and who, for many years, was the only Cardiff accent heard on radio or television.

Mitch – Refers to playing truant i.e. 'going on the mitch'.

Daps – Originally a type of canvas tennis shoe, but now commonly used to mean any type of trainer or sports footwear.

Bogey – A racing cart made from pram wheels and a plank of wood that is steered with a piece of rope and requires some poor sap, known as the 'donkey', to push it with a broom handle. Most common was the simpler to make bogey with the plank on top of the pram wheel axels, but the 'underhang' bogey has the plank attached, usually by bent nine-inch nails, underneath the axels. This provides a lower centre of gravity and allows for much faster cornering.

Dideekoy (AKA Didikoy) – This can have various different spellings and pronunciations (in Swansea they say 'didikie'). Refers to a tramp or a hobo or a derogatory term for a Gypsy. Origin is probably Romany.

Paarkeez (AKA Parkie) – Refers to a park keeper and is not, as some have mistakenly thought, the derogatory term for Pakistani.

Dowzow (AKA Dilwyn) – Refers to someone not too bright.

Nodjem – Refers to the head.

Grolup (AKA Grollop) – Refers to 'a dollop of aggro'.

Beejobuld – Refers to being frightened, shaken up or made nervous.

Dill – Short for Dilwyn (see 'dowzow' above).

Obuldeeoy (AKA Hobbledihoy, Swansea – Hobbledihi, Valleys as in, 'doing a hobble') – Refers to 'doing a fiddle', moonlighting, working for cash in hand, no tax, no questions asked. Origin probably Romany or Yiddish.

Maajorum (AKA Majorum) – Refers to a lump, load or dollop of something; as in 'have a majorum of that'.

Germojum – (AKA Germogum) – Refers to a person's mental sensibility.

Faaraawaakin boluhwoks – Refers to exactly what you think it does.

Baars – Refers to the bleating noise made by sheep.

Skin ows (AKA Skin House) – Refers to a pub (where you get a skin full).

Kaairdiff aarms paark – Refers to Cardiff Arms Park and if you're not Welsh you wouldn't understand!

Klaarksee (AKA Clarksie, Clark's Pie) – Refers to the traditional meat pie of Cardiff.

Daark (AKA Brains Dark) – Refers to what is, quite simply, the most beautiful liquid ever created.

THE FACTORY

This was originally notes for a short story that never happened. Years later I turned them into this sequence. Section 4, Snowjob was the first written when I was seventeen years old.

HOMAGE TO HENRY NORMAL

UB40 – was for many years the card you had to show when you signed on as unemployed.

Giro – A post office cheque which used to be how your Unemployment Benefit was paid.

THE GREAT RASTAFARI ANGLO-WELSH SHEEP POEM

This poem is a protest against the racism of the 1980's Anglo-Welsh poetry and literary scene. At the time of writing it, Welsh black writers were excluded from magazines and festivals in Wales by a white, middle-class arts establishment. Growing up in a multi-racial community I was very aware of this and have protested and written about it on many occasions (see my pamphlet/essay 'Radical Anti-Sheepism' for a more in-depth view). This poem was rejected by every English-language literary magazine in Wales and when I published it in my first book, I suddenly found I could no longer get work published in or do readings for any of the literary establishment magazines or festivals for at least two years.

ALAS POOR YORRICKS

Written in 1988 at the height of the HIV/AIDS crisis to lament the loss of sexual freedom and reluctantly accept the need to wear condoms.

THE POEM

'I shall play **THE THE**' – The The were a 1980's pop band.

DIS IS JEST TUH SAY LIEK

Baaraas – Refers to being really cold. Local nautical slang which comes from using a barometer. The word barometer was usually curved around the top half of the barometer's dial. When the dial's needle pointed to the 'bar' of barometer it was going to be really cold. As in, 'it's in the baras today'.

BLUE ZOBOLE

Ernest Zobole had long been one of my favourite artists when I first met him on 20th September 1994 at the opening of an exhibition of his work.

BUILDING SISYPHUS BUILDINGS

Yes I do mean 'polloping' and not plopping!

LARYNX

Written during the 1995 Hay Festival Poetry Squantum where six poets are given a word, in this case Sarajevo, with which to write a poem over the course of a weekend.

THIRTEEN WAYS OF LOOKING AT TONY CONRAN

Nigel Jenkins edited an anthology to celebrate Tony Conran and I'd written this poem for it. He put it to one side because he liked the title so much he wanted to use it for the anthology. He phoned to ask, made a note about it, we talked about a lot of other stuff, papers got moved around. The note made it into the anthology but the poem was mislaid and, in the nature of such cock-ups, it wasn't noticed until after the anthology had come out. Must be one of the very few times, if not the only time, that the title poem of an anthology was not in the anthology.

THE BOOKSHOP MANAGER'S FAREWELL

Written for Peter Finch when he stepped down as manager of Oriel, the Welsh Arts Council bookshop, after twenty-seven years.

THE LAST SWIM IN EMPIRE

About the last day in the Empire Swimming Pool, the only 50 metre pool in Cardiff when it closed, and it's also about the successful vote to have a Welsh Assembly.

TIDE MEMORY

Commissioned for the BBC Two TV documentary 'The Dock Of The Bay' in 1992 in which I was asked to imagine what Cardiff might be like after the Barrage was built. Many years later I updated the poem looking backwards at what had happened.

KAPUT

Before flat screens, televisions were huge and filled with valves and a tube which could project one to three feet backwards from the screen. If you took the cover off and touched the wrong part, even though it was unplugged, it could still give you a shock.

'FULL HOUSE'

Roofer's slang for seeing a woman totally naked.

MADOC AT THE JOBCENTRE

Madoc (AKA Madog) was a Celtic prince, the son of Owain Gwynedd who, allegedly, sailed to America in 1170 and founded a colony there. It is said that the colonists are supposed to have intermarried with local Native Americans and legend has it that their Welsh-speaking descendants still live somewhere in the United States. Many people have claimed to have found these Madocians or Manduans, but nobody has yet found any tribe that speaks Welsh.

REEMAAAARRKAAABUL

Uzzuks (AKA Uzzucks) – Refers to babies, infants or small children.

Ate o clok monstur (AKA eight o'clock monster) – Refers to the gruesome monster that comes to check that small children are in bed and asleep. Whilst on it's prowls, if it finds them out of bed and awake it eats them alive, cracking and crunching their bones and slurping their blood.

Coopeed (AKA Coupied) – To crouch down very low, as in; 'they coupied down out of sight'. Also used is 'to coupy down'.

Laarnog (AKA Larnog or Lavernock) – A place to the west and by the sea just outside Cardiff.

Klaaarksee (AKA Clarksie, Clark's Pie) – See above.

Paaarksee (AKA The Victoria Park Pie Company Mince Beef Pie (a bit of a mouthful hence the shortened version)) – These pies are made in the original Clark's bakery, were known as Clark's Pies until a split in the family, a trademark dispute and after that, there was a name change for this bakery. This pie dichotomy has divided the Cardiff pie eating community and may well lead to civil war or even a pie apocalypse. Therefore Klaaarksee or Paaarksee is a very emotionally hot topic.

Baazzee Ieelund (AKA Barry Island) – Famous funfair and seaside resort.

Aaaleekaantee (AKA Alicante) – Spanish city by the sea where the planes land for holidaymakers on their way to the exotica of Benidorm.

Gorpurs (AKA Gawpers) – Refers to eyes or looking at something, as in; 'having a good gawp', 'look at the gawpers on him' and 'what you gawping at?'

Widee (AKA Widdy) – Refers to something very small or tiny.

Dorofees (AKA Dorothy's Fish Bar) – Infamous Caroline Street chippy.

Cover Image by William Dean Ford

William Dean Ford has become more experimental with his photography since the first Lockdown in 2020. He has a long running association with the local University Health Board, and was on the committee examining submissions from artists wishing to have their work as part of the permanent art content at the (then) under construction Mental Health Unit at LLandough Hospital. Some of his words are on permanent display in the reception area as a de facto 'motto' for the facility: WE GROW BETTER TOMORROWS WHEN WE PLANT GOOD SEEDS TODAY

Since 2010 William has carved out a niche as a spoken word performer and has organised many spoken word events under his MEGAVERSE banner presenting many performers/poets. He has also produced Megaverse events for Oxfam and International Dylan Thomas Day. He lives in Cardiff.

ACKNOWLEDGEMENTS

Some of these poems have appeared in the following:

Books

Rumour Mathematics (1984)
The Bicycle Is An Easy Pancake (1986 USA, 1987 UK)
Something's Awry (1988, 1992 and 1994 UK)
Tide Memory (1992)
The Dancing Drayman (1993)
Swimming In The Living Room (1995)

Magazines and anthologies

Stride, Poetry Wales, New Welsh Review, The North, Quadrant (Australia), *Sunset* (USA), *Flat Baroque* (USA), *The Awl* (USA), *Madog, Cabaret 246, Spectrum, The Wide Skirt, The Rialto, Frames, Da Da Dance, Writing On Air, Against The Grain, Harry's Hand, Cambrensis, The Echo Room, Radical Wales, Making Waves, Y Faner Goch, The Cardiff Poet, Spokes, Spear, S.W.A.G., Orbis, Roundyhouse, The Red Poets, La Bicyclette* (France), *The Yellow Crane, CDUK, Fire, The Journal Of Anglo-Scandinavian Poetry, Scintilla, Sampler, The Pterodactyl's Wing* and *The Big Book Of Cardiff.*

Radio and television

BBC One, BBC Two, BBC Radio 4, BBC Radio Wales, HTV, ITV, Channel 4, S4C, CBC Radio, Bay FM and Red Dragon Radio.

In 2006 I was awarded an Arts Council of Wales Bursary.

Many thanks are due to my publisher Richard Davies, to my editor Suzy Wildsmith and my proof reader Gina Rathbone. Special mention here goes to Jonathan Edwards who read the book and gave me some very insightful advice.

PARTHIAN *Poetry*

Better Houses

SUSIE WILD
ISBN 978-1-912109-66-1
£8.99 | Paperback

'a new, highly distinctive and exciting poetic voice.' –
Ink Sweat & Tears

'reels gorgeously from a restaurant to the seashore to the night sky.'
– *Planet International*

'exuberant and smart […] Half-remembered, half-invented, but wholly charismatic.'
–**Wales Arts Review**

'Readers of all types will find something marvellous here.' – **Gwales**

Small

NATALIE ANN HOLBOROW
ISBN 978-1-912681-76-1
£9.99 | Paperback

'Shoot for the moon? Holborow has landed, roamed its face, dipped into the craters, and gathered an armful of stars while up there.'
– **Wales Arts Review**

'*Small* is atomic – in the best possible sense.' –
Bethany W. Pope

'Rich and visceral'
– **Kate Noakes**

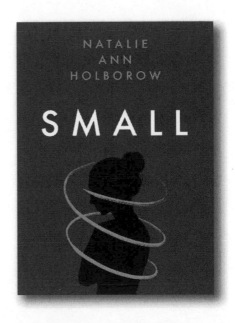

PARTHIAN *Poetry*

How to Carry Fire
Christina Thatcher
ISBN 978-1-912681-48-8
£9.00 | Paperback

'A dazzling array of poems both remarkable in their ingenuity,
and raw, unforgettable honesty.'
– Helen Calcutt

Sliced Tongue and
Pearl Cufflinks
Kittie Belltree
ISBN 978-1-912681-14-3
£9.00 | Paperback

'By turns witty and sophisticated, her writing shivers
with a suggestion of unease that is compelling.'
– Samantha Wynne-Rhydderch

Hey Bert
Roberto Pastore
ISBN 978-1-912109-34-0
£9.00 | Paperback

'Bert's writing, quite simply, makes me happy.
Jealous but happy.'
– Crystal Jeans